'This book provides valuable insights as we seek to live for God's kingdom in a world driven by consumer debt. It challenges us to look at the way in which our lifestyle choices affect other people. If we can put its message into practice, we will make a difference not only to our lives but also to the lives of many others.'

Noel Richards, songwriter and worship leader

'We need a view of life as God meant it to be lived. Both because it is what is right and true, and because it is what is best for us and our society. Guy Brandon and the Jubilee Centre are well placed to be your guides in all this. This is a most welcome summary of their thinking and I warmly commend it to you.'

Graham Beynon
Minister of Avenue Community Church, Leicester

'Provocative, persuasive and prophetic. Be prepared for a stimulating and uncomfortable read. Guy Brandon extends the Lordship of Christ to the no-go areas of money and lifestyle. This important and counter-cultural book demands nothing less than loving Christ in all we do.'

Richard M. Cunningham
Director of UCCF: The Christian Unions

'Here's a book that doesn't just present a biblical vision for a Jesus-centred ordinary life, doesn't just identify the forces of contemporary culture that are corroding our souls, poisoning our planet and fragmenting our relationships but vigorously and helpfully explores how we might actually live differently, live the life of shalom today.'

Mark Greene, Executive Director
London Institute for Contemporary Christianity

About the Jubilee Centre

The Jubilee Centre explores a wide range of social, economic and political issues, seeking to provide a positive response to the challenges faced by individuals, communities and policymakers in the twenty-first century from a distinctively faith-based perspective.

Our vision is for a movement of organizations, churches and individual Christians to advance a coherent and positively stated biblical social agenda that is of benefit to the whole of society. We believe the Bible presents a coherent social vision, based on right relationships, that provides an alternative to contemporary political ideologies. The Jubilee Centre has applied this relational agenda to areas as diverse as the economy, criminal justice, care for the elderly, asylum and immigration, the environment, and sexual ethics.

Our publications include *Just Sex: Is It Ever Just Sex?* by Guy Brandon, the ground-breaking *Jubilee Manifesto* and the quarterly *Cambridge Papers* – an influential collection of peer-reviewed studies. We also maintain an extensive blog and offer a variety of reports, videos and class/small group discussion materials on our website, most of which can be freely downloaded.

For regularly updated comment on all the issues affecting our lives and faith, visit the Jubilee Centre website at <www.jubilee-centre.org>.

To find out more, please contact us at:

Jubilee Centre
3 Hooper Street
Cambridge
CB1 2NZ

Tel: 01223 566319
Email: info@jubilee-centre.org
Website: www.jubilee-centre.org

FREE TO LIVE

*Expressing the love of Christ in
an age of debt*

Guy Brandon

First published in Great Britain in 2010

Society for Promoting Christian Knowledge
36 Causton Street
London SW1P 4ST
www.spckpublishing.co.uk

British Library Cataloguing-in-Publication Data
A catalogue record for this book is available from the British Library

ISBN 978–0–281–06229–4

1 3 5 7 9 10 8 6 4 2

Typeset by Graphicraft Ltd, Hong Kong
Printed in Great Britain by Ashford Colour Press

Produced on paper from sustainable forests

Contents

Acknowledgements

This book draws upon many years of work by the Jubilee Centre, particularly the excellent *Jubilee Manifesto* and influential and peer-reviewed quarterly publication, *Cambridge Papers*, which provide much of the original thinking and background. I am hugely grateful and indebted to those who have worked so hard before me to find practical, biblical answers to some of the biggest issues of our time.

Particular thanks go to John Hayward, Michael Schluter and Alan White for providing insight and feedback at the early stages, and to Alison Barr of SPCK for her suggestions on the final draft.

Where personal stories have been used, the names of those involved have been changed.

Introduction

We've all been through a difficult time recently. Just when things seemed to be going so well, everyone was knocked sideways by the worst recession in decades. Suddenly we found our jobs, homes and livelihoods were at risk. Yet, tough though it's been, perhaps it's also a good opportunity to rethink the way we approach life. Whatever the state of the economy, it's a comfort to remember that Jesus Christ is the same yesterday and today and for ever (Heb. 13.8).

The Bible had a way of limiting debt, poverty and inequality, namely the Jubilee year, celebrated every 50 years (Lev. 25). We don't have anything like that now, but there are still effective ways we can organize our lives to please God. For the Christian, it's our relationships that are the key to our identities – not work, money or anything else. 'Love God and love your neighbour' was how Jesus summed up the Law. This is where real life and fulfilment are to be found, and how we 'may have life, and have it to the full' (John 10.10).

The problem is that it's hard to remember that 'it is for freedom that Christ has set us free' (Gal. 5.1) when consumer culture and individualism surround us on every side. How can we possibly 'go against the flow'? How can we apply our faith in practical ways, right across every aspect of our lives? That's what this book is about: discovering an alternative to our culture's unhelpful standards, leaving us 'free to live' God's way in the big decisions as well as the small – free to live for God rather than Mammon.

Jubilee Manifesto[1] is the Jubilee Centre's definitive statement of the biblical social vision, offering a relational basis for society as a realistic and Christian alternative to other ideologies. This book is intended to complement the conceptual framework of *Jubilee Manifesto* by offering fresh insights around the practical application of relational principles to personal lifestyle in specific areas – effectively helping us create a kind of 'personal policy'. It asks how, as Christians, we should live out our faith in our day-to-day decisions. That's why, as well as the material on different areas of life, each chapter finishes with a meditation and a series of discussion questions to help readers unpack the ways in which we can use our faith to make a real difference.

Fundamentally, this book is about engaging with the issues and making deliberate, positive decisions: living on purpose, rather than living by default – indeed, living according to God's purpose, rather than living according to the world's standards. Too often Christians can use their faith as an excuse to take a step back and avoid the difficult choices, rather than allowing it to influence the whole of their lives: we fail to meet the challenge of being in the world, but not of the world (John 17.14–15). As such, we miss too many opportunities to live as God intended, to be salt and light to others, and to shape the world in which we live.

Since it is about engaging, this book intends to open up the discussion, not close it down by claiming to give final, authoritative answers. Although it tries to provide a different framework for thinking, and to suggest a range of solutions to consider, offering specific answers can be counterproductive because they often encourage people to latch on to them rather than think through the real issues properly. Simplistic answers are unhelpful, and supposedly cure-all solutions such as 'Fairtrade', 'ethical', 'energy-saving' and so on, while useful up to a point rarely get to the heart of the matter. They risk becoming unconsidered reactions if they are adopted as a panacea for problems that are far more complex and require far more of us than the mechanical, rule-based response of selecting a label: the same legalistic tendency that Jesus countered when he summarized the Law in terms of love.

As Christians living in a plural society, there is a great attraction to modelling our faith in a more rounded way than this. It is often difficult to tell the difference between the Christian life and the one our culture expects of us: the world we live in more often appears to have a greater effect on us than we have on it. Aside from how we spend our Sunday mornings, would an outside observer notice the difference between our lives and those of our neighbours?

On the other hand, what would happen if every Christian voted with his or her feet in their pursuit of whole-life discipleship? What would it be like if we knew how to apply our faith to every hour of every day – not just on Sunday morning, but to all the choices we make on a daily basis? How would our society look if we didn't settle for easy answers and superficial rules, but made decisions that reflected a true and deep desire for love, fairness and integrity – in how we work and manage our time, in what we buy, in how we spend and bank and invest, in how we treat the environment, in how we vote, in where we live, in our families, friendships and all our relationships?

> Then your light will rise in the darkness, and your night will become like the noonday. (Isa. 58.10)

John Hayward, Jubilee Centre
Cambridge

1

Free to live

———•◦•———

The kingdom of heaven is like treasure hidden in a field. When a man found it, he hid it again, and then in his joy went and sold all he had and bought that field.   *Matthew 13.44*

The parable of the hidden treasure is an image for the priceless value of a living faith. Stumbling across a forgotten hoard buried in a field, perhaps while he was working the ground to grow crops, a man seizes a once-in-a-lifetime opportunity and immediately gives up everything he owns to buy both the land and its unexpected harvest.

One moment, one opportunity, one brave and decisive action.

But selling everything to buy the field was the easy bit, even if not all of us would be so clear-thinking and strong-willed. Jesus doesn't go on to describe what the man did with his treasure after he obtained it. Did he leave it in the ground or in a bank vault for ever, or did he put it to good use? What difference did his new wealth make to his life after he bought that field?

Or moving past the imagery of the parable to the message behind it: How did his life actually *look* different after he found the kingdom of heaven?

That's the purpose of this book: to explore some of the ways in which Christianity might make a practical difference in all of our daily decisions. Its aim is to counter the idea that faith can be a bolt-on extra, confined to ring-fenced blocks of time like Sunday morning and weekly house-group, but not making much of an impact on the rest of our lives. A lot of people, Christian or otherwise, really do want to live a 'good life' – just look at the popularity of Fairtrade and other 'ethical' brands over the last few years. The problem for Christians is that the Bible doesn't always seem to give us details on *how* to do that in many of the areas of life we engage with all the time, such as the environment, how we spend our time, what we do with our money and where we shop. As a result, we can end up taking on the first promising-looking solution – energy-saving light bulbs, organic food, boycotting one or other bank.

These aren't necessarily bad in themselves, but shouldn't we be able to make a clear, distinctively Christian response to these issues – not just the 'next best thing' because the Bible doesn't immediately appear to have a good answer of its own? To adapt another of Jesus' analogies, shouldn't our faith be more like the yeast 'mixed into a large amount of flour until it worked all through the dough' (Matt. 13.33) than the jam we spread on top of the finished product, which is not integral to the bread and can be of any flavour we choose? This book is the result of years of people coming to the Jubilee Centre and asking us for a simple, Christian approach to one or other of the bewildering range of choices they make every day, in the hope of finding the one that is most pleasing to God.

But to do that – to find comprehensive, distinctively Christian solutions that speak to a wide range of important but different ethical problems – it helps to know a bit more about what it is we're really trying to fix in the first place.

An age of debt

Suddenly everyone is talking about the economy. A few years ago the dry, technical world of economics was the preserve of only a few; now everyone seems to have a reasonable grasp, at least in general terms, of what has happened. The brief version is that banks lent recklessly, and when the loans couldn't be repaid they ended up with huge but hard-to-calculate losses. As a result of their unknown liabilities they became reluctant to lend out any more money, meaning that businesses suffered and jobs were lost, leading to the worst recession since the Great Depression. (How this happened is explored in more detail in Appendix 1: Background to the financial crisis.)

But although we all know about 'subprime mortgages' and 'toxic debt', fewer people are asking *why* this occurred – not just in relatively superficial terms about the economy, but in terms of what it tells us about our underlying cultural attitudes and the personal values that determine how we approach the world as a whole. Because although our values inevitably determine what we do with our income, those same tendencies result in far wider problems than just the 'credit crunch'. They affect the way we act in *every* area of life – how we spend our money, how we use our time, our romantic relationships, how we treat the environment, even how we see ourselves. For the Christian, this can raise some awkward questions about the different rivals for our worship – cash, work, sex, possessions, pride and many others too numerous to list.

Jesus often uses debt as an image for sin, as in the parable of the unmerciful servant (Matt. 18.21–35), who chases a fellow servant for a small debt even though their master has just forgiven him a huge, unpayable debt. That's why the Lord's Prayer reads 'forgive us our debts, as we also have forgiven our debtors' (Matt. 6.12).

It's also the reason this book is called *Free to Live: Expressing the love of Christ in an age of debt.* Money isn't the only way we can get into 'debt'. The way we treat the environment, our time, sometimes even our closest relationships, is like storing up debt that will, sooner or later, have to be repaid – whether that's in the fossil fuels we won't have in 40 years because we burned too much of them now, or the partner we love but will separate from in five years because we didn't invest in the right areas of the relationship at the start.

But there's a little more to it than that. Although the credit crunch and recession that followed have been serious, they were only the tip of the iceberg, a symptom of a much deeper problem that affects all of these areas, described in more detail below. In that sense, the financial crisis was a wake-up call. People realized that we can't treat debt the same way any more, and changed – or were forced to change – the way they lived. But the real challenge is to take the opportunity to make similar changes elsewhere in our lives. Since the economy turned a corner and is apparently on the road to recovery,[1] this challenge has become even more acute: will it be back to 'business as usual', or will we learn from the mistakes of the past, in the economy and in other areas?

Behind the scenes

America's credit crunch is putting the squeeze on the marriages of New York's superwealthy as a record number of couples with $10 million or more in assets sue for divorce.

Lisa Thomas, a family therapist, based in Denver, Colorado, has noticed how love among the rich can ebb when the money falls short. 'If you don't have a pony show going on 24/7 you have to look at the relationship and that can be very scary. The toys were a distraction, but now they may be running out and, though once we used to love each other, I'm not sure if we do anymore', Ms Thomas said.

Not that anyone would admit their divorce is motivated by money, probably not even to themselves. Mr Felder, who represented Rudolph Giuliani, the former Mayor of New York in his recent divorce, and Mike Tyson's former wife, Robin Given, in hers, said: 'Money's really all that it's about, the husbands know it, but the wives will never say it. I've been doing this for years. I know, the judge knows, though you can't prove it.'[2]

The credit crunch – or perhaps more accurately 'debt disaster' – seemed to come out of the blue for all but a tiny minority of critics who claimed to have foreseen and warned against it, and an even smaller minority who anticipated it and used the opportunity to profit from it. While savers and those who lost their jobs suffered badly in the recession, others benefited unexpectedly as interest rates plummeted and tracker mortgages became cheaper and cheaper. But earlier examples show that the housing bubble and other conditions that led to the credit crunch were not an isolated event – despite the fact that this time it was a particularly severe 'correction'. Looking further back, these bubbles and crashes have occurred repeatedly throughout history. They are easy to identify in retrospect, far harder to predict. The 'tulip mania' of seventeenth-century Holland was probably the first. Investors bought and sold tulip bulbs at ever higher prices, equivalent to years of wages, until the market suddenly collapsed. Two other early examples were the South Sea Bubble in 1720, in which investors sought to take advantage of South Sea Company's supposedly exclusive trading rights with Spain's South American colonies, and speculation on Britain's growing railway network in the 1840s, while more recent ones include Japanese asset prices in the 1980s and the dot-com bubble of the late 1990s.

It's tempting to write off the credit crunch, and any speculative bubble, as the result of nothing more than greed. But while it certainly plays a part, greed alone doesn't reach the heart of what the credit crunch and recession tell us about our society and about

> *'Anyone who believes exponential growth can go on for ever in a finite world is either a madman or an economist.'*
> Kenneth Boulding, economist and philosopher

ourselves. The debt disaster was only one consequence of a deeper problem; it was a serious outcome, but a symptom rather than a cause in itself. If we ignore the underlying cause in favour of the easy answer of greed, we risk limiting the lessons we can learn; we risk limiting the outcome to making simplistic changes to our lives instead of addressing the root illness.

A nation of consumers

Os Guinness tells the story of Petrov, a dockyard worker in communist Russia. Because wages were so low, employees would steal anything they could, and KGB agents were stationed at the exits to search them as they left. Every day, Petrov would wheel a barrow full of sawdust out through the gate. The guard would search it and find nothing. Several weeks passed, until in his frustration, the guard finally promised that he wouldn't arrest him, if he only told him what it was he was stealing. Petrov replied, 'Wheelbarrows'.

In his book, *Disciples and Citizens*, Graham Cray uses this story to illustrate how it is easy to miss the real problem – in this case the 'consumerization' of our lives – in our attention to the obvious issues.[3] Crucially, 'consumerism' in this sense does not just mean spending money to own more things. Although that's one side of it, more significantly it points to an underlying attitude in the way we approach the world.

Some of the conditions that made the financial crisis possible, while not necessarily bad in themselves and often beneficial, can have terrible effects on other areas of our lives. Improvements in communication and travel have vastly increased the possibilities for global trade, but they have also led to people moving around a lot more, meaning that they are separated from their families and the communities into which they were born. People move further and more often, friendships and other relationships are stretched, and family breakdown increases. Isolation and often loneliness are the result.

Given how isolated many people feel, it's no coincidence that we have adopted a more individualistic outlook. Individualism is the mindset that says that I can live my life on my own terms, without reference to others; I make my own choices and, so long as I don't hurt anyone else in the process, no one has the right to criticize me for them. This 'me culture' naturally emphasizes my individual rights above my wider responsibilities to friends, family, local and work communities and society as a whole. It also fails to understand how important these relationships are for my well-being, and how my actions affect others because they are a part of the society in which we all live. Instead, relationships tend to become confused and redefined. They become 'me-centred' – whatever I want or need them to be for me at the time. Individualism is a blindness to the idea that people live interconnected lives; an assumption of independence and a denial of interdependence. It says that my 'real' identity is to be found within myself and my own choices, not expressed through society's many mutual, outward relationships.

Consumerism is the natural counterpart of this tendency. Individualism encourages isolation, and consumerism fills the search for meaning and identity that results. Graham Cray writes, 'If individualization creates the structure of our society, consumerism provides its dominant ideology and its navigation mechanism or satellite navigation mechanism. Individuals navigate a multichoice world by being consumers.'[4] In other words, we have come to understand ourselves through consumption – what we buy, what we 'buy into' or the values and ideas we adopt and, perhaps most importantly, through what we *desire*. Relationships are reduced to how they suit me; our internal, personal choices are what tell us and others who we are, not our place in families and other networks of belonging.

Choice and therefore change are fundamental to consumerism, as is dissatisfaction: if we are happy with what we have, we won't want to acquire anything new. And consumerism does not apply solely to the things we buy. As we shall see, it's a mindset that extends to almost every area of our lives – to the relational, sexual and environmental as much as to the material. Chapter 8 looks further at how this applies even to the way we see ourselves and choose our own identities.

> '*Choice itself becomes the good, novelty usurps beauty, and subject-ive experiences displace truth.*' Pope Benedict XVI[5]

Seen in these terms, cheap credit and lax regulation are only contri-buting factors to a problem caused by what amounts to a misplaced identity. We want choice, we want change, we want the option to be or feel or do something different. Easy credit just gives us the oppor-tunity to buy it.

The Jubilee year

Early drafts of this book were entitled 'Jubilee Lifestyle' because it grew out of an earlier Jubilee Centre publication, *Jubilee Manifesto*. The *Manifesto* describes a relational framework for Christian social reform, which this book applies on a personal level. The Jubilee was supposed to be hugely important in the life of Old Testament Israel. Understanding how and why this was the case underpins a lot of the Jubilee Centre's work (hence the name). Despite the fact that Leviticus 25 was written around 3,000 years ago, the Jubilee year was one of the most important ways that God ensured that relationships between families and communities were maintained and strengthened, and has far-reaching implications for the way we choose to live our lives today.

Every seventh day in Israel was a Sabbath (Exod. 20.8–11). On this day, no one was to work and no one could force anyone else to work either – even a slave or a foreigner (Exod. 20.10). The Israelites had once been slaves in Egypt, and the Sabbath rest was a reminder of God's grace in bringing them out of oppression under Pharaoh (Deut. 5.15).

Every seventh year was a 'Sabbath year', a special year in which the land was to rest and there was no sowing or reaping. All debts were to be cancelled, and anyone who had sold himself into slavery because of hardship or to pay a debt was to be freed (Lev. 25.1–7; Deut. 15.1–11). What this effectively meant was that crippling debt and long-term poverty should not have been features of Israelite life: there was a limit to financial hardship.

Finally, every seventh Sabbath year was a Jubilee year, a kind of 'super Sabbath' (Lev. 25.8–54). In this year, as well as allowing the land to rest, cancelling debts and releasing slaves, every family was to return to its ancestral property – the land that each family had originally been given when the Israelites first entered the Promised Land. The Law stated that land in Israel could not be bought or sold permanently, only purchased on a leasehold basis for use until the next Jubilee, when it reverted to its original owners. This meant that not only were debts written off, but every family would have access to the means of production again, giving them a new chance of economic independence. The Jubilee year also strengthened communities and family ties, because one of the reasons a person might leave their family home was poverty. In times of hardship, a man might be forced to sell his land and work for someone else – perhaps on the very land he had sold. But without support from family and friends, he might have to move to find work, away from the community in which he grew up. 'If one of your countrymen becomes poor and is unable to support himself among you, help him as you would an alien or a temporary resident, so he can continue to live among you' (Lev. 25.35).

So the Sabbath, Sabbath year and Jubilee year were a range of measures to encourage justice in work relationships, to limit debt and poverty to a relatively short period of time, to ensure economic independence and to strengthen families and local communities. It prevented the wealthy from amassing large tracts of land and oppressing the poor.

In the Bible, debt was seen as undesirable. Taking a loan was a last-ditch solution to financial hardship. Paying debts was taken seriously; if a debt could not be repaid, a man might have to sell himself into slavery to work for the lender until the debt was paid off – though 'slaves' in Israel were actually indentured labourers, far better treated and with more rights than in other neighbouring cultures (Lev. 25.39–40). But debt was taken seriously from the lender's point of view too: it was not supposed to be a money-making opportunity. Those who lent money were instructed to do so as an act of compassion and not to take advantage of their poor neighbour by charging interest (Exod. 22.25; Lev. 25.35–37; Deut. 23.19).

Sadly, there is little or no evidence that the Jubilee year was ever fully observed in Old Testament times – in fact, Isaiah criticizes those 'who add house to house and join field to field' (Isa. 5.8), amassing land and fortunes but living immorally and denying others justice in their pursuit of wealth (5.23). Although there are some records of the land being allowed to lie fallow every seventh year throughout Israel's history, by New Testament times the rabbis had created legal processes to circumvent the forgiveness of debt that was also supposed to occur, and the extent to which slaves were released is uncertain too.

The point remains that the Bible's view of debt is very different from our own, modern approach. What was then seen as a last resort in circumstances of dire need is now an integral part of life – our economy simply wouldn't function without it, as we very nearly found out in 2008. Charging interest was seen as unjust – as bad as robbery (Ezek. 18). Now, interest-bearing loans are seen, at best, as a necessary evil – few people would be able to buy a house without a mortgage. At worst, debt is a way of extending our income, deferring payment for a lifestyle we cannot currently afford.

> High earners are struggling with debt as much as people on low incomes, according to financial experts and advisory charities. The withdrawal of easy credit as a result of the credit crunch has forced even those earning six-figure salaries to seek help with their debts, one debt management company says.
>
> Michael, a company director who earns nearly £70,000, is in this position. He has four children, the eldest of whom is now at university, and over the years has built up £39,000 credit card debt, £20,000 on a personal loan, a £5,000 overdraft and a £150,000 mortgage. He took out his credit cards when they were offering zero per cent interest deals, but these have now ended and he is unable to get more credit to consolidate his debts. He is struggling to meet the monthly payments or the day-to-day spending needed to keep his family going. He is making no inroads into his borrowings and is now waiting to hear whether his creditors will accept his suggestion of freezing interest on the outstanding debt. His mortgage lender has refused to extend his home loan as 'it isn't their policy to lend for consolidation because their experience is that people build up the debt again'.
>
> Michael denies that he has been profligate: 'Some people said how did we manage to rack up these debts on the income we're on. But we have a mortgage, bills, four children and I've paid 40 per cent in tax for ten years. I don't think I have an excessive lifestyle. The money has gone on general expenditure: we don't have lots of holidays abroad,

we don't buy expensive clothes. If we've had a holiday it's been Center Parcs for a week.'

He admits that when he and his partner have bought things for the house, they have been of good quality; he did buy a nice car when he last changed jobs, and the household has had three or four Xboxes and PlayStations. He also admits that he has never saved for anything: 'If the kids needed a new laptop I wouldn't think anything about ordering it straight away and putting it on my credit card.'[6]

Excessive debt is the natural counterpart of consumerism. If it's true that 'individualization creates the structure of our society' and 'consumerism provides its . . . satellite navigation mechanism',[7] then debt is the fuel that keeps the engine moving. Without access to credit, the urge towards consumption would be choked. Available credit allows us to distance our consumer lifestyles from our work and earnings. It sends the message: 'If you want something, have it – now.' The grounds for the decision to buy something move away from being able to afford it towards wanting or 'deserving' it. The message of consumerism is that life should fit me – suiting my needs is just a matter of making the right choices. Debt allows us to access new choices. It shifts the balance away from the constraints of my circumstances and financial means – how I fit in with the world – on to the ways that the world could 'serve' me.

The result of our voracious appetite for credit was the near-collapse of the banking system and the worst recession in 70 years. Our indebted culture has a love–hate relationship with debt: for all the goods it provides us with, its effects can quickly turn from opportunity to personal and national tragedy. Payment is only ever deferred, and thanks to compound interest the cost will always be higher than the nominal amount (pay off a £3,000 credit card bill at a relatively standard rate of 19.9 per cent interest, with minimum repayments of 2 per cent or £5, whichever is greater, and the total cost will be over £12,000). But this is not the only way in which consumerism encourages us to mortgage our futures. Relief from financial debt was integral to the Jubilee, but so was relief from wider relational poverty. The message of 'take now and pay later' applies to other areas explored in this book, perhaps most significantly sex and the environment. We use natural resources faster than they can be replaced, fuelling our current lifestyles but damaging our relationships in the process and storing up problems for the near future. Similarly, sex is treated as a consumer commodity, a mindset that typically doesn't consider that it might be undermining to other relationships, including any long-term, stable future partnership to which we may aspire. Even our time itself is consumerized, costed and allocated but not truly valued in the process.

Instead of understanding ourselves in terms of our families, communities, relationships and perhaps our work, consumerism tells us that our identity is based on what we consume in different ways – materially, culturally, ideologically, and even in our relationships themselves. By contrast, Christianity looks at life in terms of relationships. Rather than seeing the world in terms of 'me', it only ever views 'me' as one half of a relationship – the other half being God, or another person or group of people. They're two very different ways of looking at the world, with two very different outcomes. The next chapter looks at a biblical, relational way of approaching the whole of life, as an antidote to our culture's corrosive consumerism and as a fresh way of looking at the ethical issues to which people desperately want answers.

Meditation

Therefore, I urge you, brothers, in view of God's mercy, to offer your bodies as living sacrifices, holy and pleasing to God – this is your spiritual act of worship. Do not conform any longer to the pattern of this world, but be transformed by the renewing of your mind. Then you will be able to test and approve what God's will is – his good, pleasing and perfect will. (Rom. 12.1–2)

Discussion questions

- What are the areas in which you think consumer culture most affects the Church and individual Christian life?
- From a consumer-culture point of view, what is attractive about that way of living?
- What are the downsides?

2

Expressing the love of Christ in an age of debt

—•◆•—

God does not play dice with the universe; He plays an ineffable game of His own devising, which might be compared, from the perspective of the players (i.e. everybody), to being involved in an obscure and complex version of poker in a pitch-dark room, with blank cards, for infinite stakes, with a Dealer who won't tell you the rules, and who smiles all the time.
Terry Pratchett and Neil Gaiman, Good Omens[1]

Whereas the last chapter looked at individualism and its counterpart, consumerism – the framework through which our culture typically approaches the world – this chapter looks at a Christian response to the problems of how to navigate the 'me culture' and how to make decisions that reflect a concern to live for Christ in every area of life.

This is important for more than one reason. James argues that, although we are ultimately justified by faith, our actions are a crucial barometer of how seriously we take that faith (James 2.14–26). In addition, it's sometimes hard to see how Christians' lives are much different from anyone else's – except, perhaps, for a brief hour or two on a Sunday morning. In Matthew 5.13–15, Jesus encourages the Church to be salt and light to others, 'that they may see your good deeds and praise your Father in heaven'. How Christians act in their everyday lives is a powerful witness to society: the sincerity and relevance of their faith is often judged solely on the visible difference it makes.

Why relationships?

As suggested by the quote at the beginning of the chapter, Christians and non-Christians alike can often find it hard to believe that there might be good reasons behind some of the Bible's laws. The Old

Testament's teachings, in particular, can seem completely arbitrary and irrelevant to the concerns of real life (avoiding wearing clothes made of different fabrics and not clipping the edge of the beard – Leviticus 19.19 and 27 – are two that stand out in terms of strangeness). No wonder that some people's resulting idea of God is of a distant figure who makes up odd or impossible standards for us, for no other reason than to see whether or not we will show him loyalty by following them.

But while some of the Bible's laws initially appear to have little of use to say to twenty-first-century Western society, they are not arbitrary. It's easy to see the Bible, especially the Old Testament, as a series of dry rules, created for a time and people so far removed from our present world that it's too much of a stretch to extract any relevance from them. But that's a reading that misses the point – and, in the process, reduces God in our minds to a harsh and vindictive character who demands obedience to laws we cannot understand or keep.

When Jesus was asked what was the greatest commandment, he responded:

> 'Love the Lord your God with all your heart and with all your soul and with all your mind.' This is the first and greatest commandment. And the second is like it: 'Love your neighbour as yourself.' All the Law and the Prophets hang on these two commandments.
>
> (Matthew 22.34–40)

Rather than answering in terms of punishment or obligation, his reply was stated in terms of relationships: not 'Don't murder', or 'Keep the Sabbath holy', but 'Love God and love your neighbour, because that's what *everything else* is designed to achieve.' This provides a startlingly different perspective from the understanding of God as a remote and secretive poker player.

Imagine studying a document that contains precise instructions for painting a series of lines on a surface: colour, spacing, position, length, single or double. Without full information about what the surface is to be used for, such instructions might seem arbitrary and unnecessarily detailed. Maybe you'd think that the colour wasn't actually that important, or that a single line would be just as visible as two parallel ones. But as soon as you learn that the surface is a road, such a document takes on a whole new significance. The lines are there for a reason, and drivers don't just follow the rules they represent for fear of being prosecuted. The person who wrote the document had something more important in mind than that – namely safety, fairness and efficiency for the drivers.

Dale Kuehne writes:

> Christianity is not a religion created by a persnickety God who plays 'gotcha' with his creation by creating a maze of countless rules and regulations and then takes pleasure in punishing each and every misstep. Christianity is actually a dramatic love story between God and his creation. While biblical law plays an important role in the love story, it is a supporting role. Even the Ten Commandments are fundamentally about two things: how to love God and how to love one other. Every law in the entire Bible is about one or the other. Why? Men and women were created for the purpose of relating with God and one another. The health of our relationships is the central concern of the law. The story of the Bible is the story of God creating us for relationship, our breaking off that relationship, and God offering to redeem it.[2]

Christianity: a relational religion

It may come as a surprise to some people that Christianity is a religion with a concern for right relationships at its heart. But God is, in his very nature, relational. In the Trinity, three distinct persons are in an equal and eternal relationship of love. When God created humankind, he did so in his own image (Gen. 1.26) – and as God's image-bearers on earth, the capacity, need and desire for relationship is built into us. It's fundamental to being human.

The Torah – the Law given by God to the people of Israel and recorded in the first five books of the Bible – contains 613 rules. Each is stated either positively ('keep the Sabbath holy', 'love your neighbour') or negatively ('do not murder', 'do not hold back payment of wages'), but every single one was concerned to promote love and maintain justice in some aspect of the relationships of the Israelite people, in the ways they interacted with God, with each other, and with those of other nations and religions. The way society was structured was intended to point to and reflect God's relational character, and the Law was part of the way this was supposed to be achieved.

In the New Testament, Jesus argued that the Law was still valid and relevant: 'Do not think that I have come to abolish the Law or

the Prophets; I have not come to abolish them but to fulfil them'
(Matt. 5.17). In practice, this means that some laws remained the
same (such as 'do not steal'); some were completed and surpassed by
his crucifixion (such as the laws requiring daily blood sacrifice);
and some remained but in a different form ('you have heard that
it was said to the people long ago, "Do not break your oath . . ."
But I tell you, Do not swear at all . . .' – see Matt. 5.33–34). Nevertheless, the purpose behind the Law remained the same, and as important as ever. When Jesus said that he did not come to abolish the
Law, he might as well have said he did not come to abolish love,
justice and right relationships – the foundations on which the
Law rested.

Viewed in these terms, the crucifixion was God's ultimate relational
act, restoring the broken relationship between him and his creation,
once and for all. The writer of Hebrews expresses in some detail the
provisional nature of the Law, which pointed forward to Jesus for its
completion:

> The law is only a shadow of the good things that are coming – not the
> realities themselves. For this reason it can never, by the same sacrifices
> repeated endlessly year after year, make perfect those who draw near
> to worship. If it could, would they not have stopped being offered?
> For the worshippers would have been cleansed once for all, and would
> no longer have felt guilty for their sins. But those sacrifices are an
> annual reminder of sins, because it is impossible for the blood of
> bulls and goats to take away sins. Therefore, when Christ came into
> the world, he said:
>
> 'Sacrifice and offering you did not desire,
>   but a body you prepared for me;
> with burnt offerings and sin offerings
>   you were not pleased.
> Then I said, "Here I am – it is written about me in the scroll –
>   I have come to do your will, O God."'
>
> First he said, 'Sacrifices and offerings, burnt offerings and sin offerings
> you did not desire, nor were you pleased with them' (although the law
> required them to be made). Then he said, 'Here I am, I have come to
> do your will.' He sets aside the first to establish the second. And by
> that will, we have been made holy through the sacrifice of the body of
> Jesus Christ once for all.   (Hebrews 10.1–10)

Law and relationship

It can be easy for us to read the Bible, particularly the Old Testament, and assume that its religion is about little more than rules – a long list of laws we either do or do not comply with, get right or wrong – and that God is pleased with us or otherwise depending on how we score. The Old Testament prophets found that they continually had to correct the same misunderstanding. Again and again they had to remind the people of Israel and Judah that mechanically following the Law wasn't what God asked of them. Their listeners often thought they would receive God's blessing if they went through the motions, carrying out sacrifices and keeping his Commandments, without really questioning *why* they were there in the first place. We can often share their legalistic, box-ticking understanding of religion; arguably the only difference is that our response to this dry, heartless form of religion is to leave the rules behind, rather than follow them regardless.

Either response misses the point. The Law shows the boundaries of how we should act, and is a signpost to its creator, but what God really wants from us is something that cannot be achieved through lawmaking. Micah 6.8 reads, 'He has shown you, O man, what is good. And what does the Lord require of you? To act justly and to love mercy and to walk humbly with your God.'

> I think I'm a good person – better than a lot of my friends. I don't break the law, except for speeding occasionally. I give to charity. I help other people. I don't lie or steal – I don't even fiddle my tax return. I think God, if there is a God, would be pleased with me.[3]

The Talmud, a collection of Jewish teachers' discussions around the Law, records the story of a Gentile who approached the influential first-century rabbi Shammai and told him that he would convert to Judaism if Shammai could teach him the whole of the Torah while the man stood on one foot. Shammai, who was famous for his strict interpretations of the law and his often irritable temperament, chased him away with a stick. The Gentile then went to Shammai's contemporary, Hillel, another influential rabbi well known for his milder interpretations and his humility, and made the same request. Hillel's response was, 'What is hateful to you, do not to your neighbour. That is the whole Torah, while the rest is the commentary; go and learn it.'[4]

Like Jesus and like Micah, Hillel's understanding of faith in action was intensely practical. It was not primarily about fulfilling lists of criteria and following obscure laws, but about seeking right relationships. If we look to the Bible for guidance we often expect a response like Shammai's, whereas the reality is quite different. Instead of a list of 'dos and don'ts', Jesus' answer is, 'Love God, and love your neighbour.'

From right to left

The idea of right relationships provides a positive, comprehensive framework for interpreting and applying biblical teaching. Every single law in the Bible is, as Dale Kuehne writes, either about loving God or loving our neighbour. They all seek to address some aspect of one or other relationship. One of the reasons we assume many biblical laws are irrelevant is that we do not know to which aspect of which relationship they apply. Once we discover what different laws were supposed to achieve for their original listeners, we can understand the intention behind them and what continuing relevance they still have for us. Like the Hebrew language in which the Old Testament is written, we need to read the Bible 'from right to left'; we need to understand it in its own context before we apply it to our own.[5]

This is something that most people accept at some level. Although there are many laws that seem unimportant or even offensive to us, and can perhaps be attributed to some quirk or circumstance of their time, others clearly still hold true, and always will. Most of the Ten Commandments – including murder, theft and lying – fall into this category. The problem is that for every obvious case, there are others that are harder to understand. So the question becomes not whether we should accept or reject the Old Testament's laws as a whole, but where to draw the line.

The Old Testament contains laws that speak to a broad range of relationships – economic, political, religious and sacrificial, agricultural and geographical, within families, with foreign countries and cultures, and more. As Christians, as well as understanding the significance these had in their original setting, we need to view them through the teaching of the New Testament. The questions are whether Jesus' coming has altered Old Testament laws and if so, how.

For example, as the writer of Hebrews explains, Jesus was the perfect sacrifice for sin, so any further sacrifice in the Temple would be redundant. This does not mean that we are no longer required to make sacrifices of *any* kind (whether of time, money or possessions – the spirit of the Law), only that the old system of animal sacrifice (the letter of the law) is now obsolete. Just because the Temple has been destroyed doesn't mean that we shouldn't express our gratitude to God in other ways. Similarly, the purpose of some Old Testament laws seems to have been to symbolize and encourage Israel's identity as separate from the surrounding nations. These laws highlighted the Israelites' own unique religious identity, or prevented them from taking on certain cultural practices that were linked to religious rites of their neighbours that could have led them away from God. Because Jesus' death removed the barrier between Jew and Gentile (Gal. 3.26–29), many of these specific laws no longer apply; hence Christians today eat pork and shellfish (see also Mark 7.14–19) and wear clothes of mixed fabrics. However, we are to remain distinct from our surrounding culture in how we think, speak and act (Mark 7.20–22).

In other cases, such as for the Ten Commandments, Jesus affirms Old Testament standards without altering them – or even strengthens them by explaining the principle behind them and drawing the line further back. So murder is against the Law, but Jesus warns against anger, which can lead to violence. Adultery is against the law, but he warns against lust, the attitude of the heart on which it depends (Matt. 5.21–30). In the case of divorce, which was permitted by Deuteronomy 24.1–4, he explains that this was a concession to imperfect circumstances – the 'least-worst' solution – and not God's ideal for long-term, committed relationships (Matt. 19.3–12).

The purpose of the Old Testament laws was to create a healthy society held together by strong relationships of all kinds, and one that recognized God as the centre of corporate and individual lives. The way we understand and apply the law as Christians should have the same objectives. That's what this book is all about.

Relational well-being

As Christianity is a relational religion, it should come as no surprise to discover that, by every available measure, relationships are what actually make us happy – not vast amounts of cash. Richard Layard of the London School of Economics writes:

> People in the West have got no happier in the last 50 years. They have become much richer, they work much less, they have longer holidays, they travel more, they live longer, and they are healthier. But they are no happier.[6]

In our commercialized and individualistic culture it's easy to assume that money or economic growth are the answers, or that I am self-sufficient and autonomous – that I depend on no one and affect no one else with my own behaviour, and that I am responsible for my own happiness. Of course, precisely the reverse is true: we can only understand ourselves through our interactions, not apart from them – in our relationships with other people, with our work, through all our give-and-take exchanges with the world around us. Suggesting otherwise is like the Zen riddle that asks, 'What is the sound of one hand clapping?' Ignoring this reality not only misses the truth – it actually closes the door on the wealth of relationships on which our happiness depends.

Life can look very different depending on whether we view it through an individualistic or relational lens, and so can many of the decisions we make and the technologies we consume. Even choices that seem relatively minor or routine can lead to different outcomes, depending on the framework within which we apply them.[7] Take 'new media', a collection of technologies that have revolutionized communication over the last 15 years. Mobile phones, email, social networking sites like Facebook and Twitter, blogs and RSS feeds have made mass exchange of data instant, global and interactive. It has never been easier to send and access information. However, our lives may be relationally richer or poorer as a result, depending on how we use them. Sending an email is far quicker and easier than writing a letter, for example, and achieves more or less the same ends without the built-in cost, delay and chances of getting lost in the post (though emails can also go astray). On the other hand, few people could claim they haven't wasted time web-surfing or reading relatively unimportant emails that, with hindsight, they might have better spent in person with friends or family. As a self-confessed Facebook 'addict' put it:

As a newbie to online social networking, my first few forays into Facebook had been cautious and brief. It had been a guilty pleasure – an enjoyable escape which tapped into a basic urge to share and compare. But over two years, I'd turned into a Facebook fiend, uploading over 30 photograph albums, posting countless inane status updates and acquiring hundreds of online 'friends' (350, to be exact). I'd got sucked into semi-stalkerdom and felt something akin to separation anxiety if I ever found myself offline for more than a few hours. What had been my favourite waste of time had morphed into a demanding and anti-social addiction.

The turning point came when I completely forgot about a long-planned reunion with a friend one evening because I'd been sidetracked by mindless Facebook mulling. This is ridiculous, I thought. Surely social networking was supposed to enhance my social life, not to trash it?[8]

Even apart from the time and cost savings such technologies can represent, the way we engage with them can support or hinder our relationships. Social networking sites can be used to make contact with huge lists of 'friends' or 'followers', nominally allowing us to maintain perhaps hundreds of relationships on a superficial level without deepening any of them, like a juggler keeping a number of balls in the air without holding on to any for more than a moment. Alternatively, it can be used to complement our 'real' relationships – to check in with people, arrange face-to-face meetings and build intimacy. The reality, of course, will usually be somewhere between the two, but the relational benefits and risks are worth bearing in mind when we sign up to such services. One way or another, almost every decision we make has some effect on our relationships.

Free to live

So as well as providing a key for understanding the often obscure world of Old Testament laws, the biblical concern for right relationships with God and other people offers us a handle on the complexities of modern ethical issues. Relational thinking is a language that everyone can relate to, whether they have a faith or not. For that reason, it's useful for apologetics – the technical term for the area of theology that seeks to defend the Christian worldview – as it gives some common ground to discuss the lifestyle choices with which we are faced on a daily basis. It gives us a vital premise upon which to weigh up those choices, some of which are included in the topics explored in this book. Without such a biblically grounded standard we are left with inconsistent or subjective justifications for our decisions, and without an overall framework to assess overlapping and sometimes apparently conflicting areas. For example, should I buy Fairtrade or organic – or save the extra it will cost and give it to charity? Should I get married, or is moving in together enough of a commitment? Which option should I take for investing any spare money – bank account, shares, pension provisions, tax-free savings, health insurance . . . or is there something better? How should I engage with environmental issues? Above all, what is distinctive and special about the Christian answer to these questions?

This book is about finding new ways to honour God in the decisions that make up our everyday existences. It's about discovering that 'Jubilee lifestyle' or 'whole-life worship': understanding what God really wants from us and trying to put it into practice in everything we do, across our public as well as private lives. It's about applying God's wisdom to what it means to love our neighbour, which includes a sense of responsibility for others as well as an element of celebration and thanksgiving, in the small stuff as much as the big events of life – whether it's buying a new house for £200,000 or a cup of coffee for £2. And it's about living lives of integrity that appeal to those around us as part of our Christian witness.

Meditation

> Trust in the LORD with all your heart and lean not on your own understanding; in all your ways acknowledge him, and he will make your paths straight. (Prov. 3.5–6)

Discussion questions

- What are the areas of your life that you currently think are difficult to relate to your faith?
- Are there other areas you would like to use to honour God, if you could?
- Why do you think these areas are 'outside of your faith' at the moment?

3

Time is money?

A wealthy businessman was grabbing a late lunch in between meetings from a street hot-dog vendor, who was just starting to pack up his stall for the day.

'You're finishing already?' he said.

'That's right.'

'But why? It's only 2.30 p.m.'

'Because I've sold all the hot dogs I need to support my family for now.'

'What are you going to do the rest of the day?'

'Well, I'll head home, spend some time with my wife and have a cup of coffee. Then I'll collect the kids from school, maybe help them with their homework and take them out to play in the park. In the evening I'll relax with friends.'

'But you could do so much better!' replied the businessman. 'Listen, if you worked a few hours more, you could catch the evening rush too. You might double your profits. You could use the extra money to buy another cart and hire someone to staff it. You could branch out, get sponsorship from local businesses – soon you could have hot-dog carts all over the city. After a few years you could sell it all on to someone else for hundreds of thousands of pounds.'

'And what would I do then?' asked the man.

'Well . . . then you could retire. Relax, play with your children, spend time with your wife and friends.'[1]

Time is arguably our most precious resource. Once it's gone, it's gone, and no matter what we do, we cannot squeeze more than 24 hours into a day. The more demands we have on our time, the more valuable the remaining hours and minutes become. Unfortunately, this indisputable fact often conflicts with the goal of cultivating right relationships, with God and other people. In prioritizing the relationships that matter most, time is the crucial factor.

> 'For disappearing acts, it's hard to beat what happens to the eight
> hours supposedly left after eight of sleep and eight of work.'
>
> Doug Larson, journalist

Mobile phones, email and social networking sites make it easier than ever before to stay in touch, but when it comes to maintaining meaningful relationships, there's no substitute for spending time with someone in person. 'Time is the currency of relationships,'[2] and our strict temporal budget of 86,400 seconds per day is subject to heavy competition.

Work takes one of the largest slices of our time: a third or more of every Monday to Friday might be spent at our jobs. That's almost a quarter of our total adult lives until retirement. But although the 'long-hours' culture means we might work more than in the recent past, working hours now are much lower compared to some other periods of history. During the Industrial Revolution it was common for people to work 14 hours a day, six days a week – more than twice today's average. The Factory Act of 1874 limited working hours to 56.5 hours per week. The 1833 Act had established a 48-hour-per-week limit – for 10–13-year-olds!

Over recent decades, rising wages have meant that despite working less, we are still far wealthier than before. Since the 1970s, the UK's Gross Domestic Product (GDP) has doubled, though this doesn't necessarily prove anything in terms of our overall well-being. GDP is an economic indicator alone. If you pay someone to do your childcare and they pay you to do theirs, GDP goes up with no real benefit to either of you. Worse, GDP includes unsustainable spending habits; take the car to work instead of walking and you increase the country's GDP in the cost of fuel and maintenance, but at the expense of increased pollution and poorer health. Criticizing GDP as a sole measure of the well-being of a country, one columnist writes:

> We're in an economic hole, and as we climb out, what we need is not simply a measurement of how much money passes through our hands each quarter, but an indicator that will tell us if we are really and truly gaining ground in the perennial struggle to improve the material conditions of our lives.[3]

And as Bill Bryson puts it:

> Thanks to all that hard work, America as a nation produces twice the goods and services per person that it produced in 1948. Everyone in the country could, in principle at least, work a four-hour day or a six-month year and still maintain a standard of living equivalent to that enjoyed by our parents. Almost uniquely among the developed nations, America took none of its productivity gains in additional leisure. It bought consumer items instead.[4]

Rising GDP hasn't bought us more quality time. More money means bigger houses to look after, but it turns out that people actually spend less time on housework than 30 years ago.[5] However, more disposable income also means more distractions. The average person in the UK watches TV for 25 hours a week, or three and a half hours a day, and one in five spend 36 hours or more a week in front of the TV – more hours than many people work.[6] So perhaps we're not all quite as short on time as we think. What would life be like if we limited our TV and internet use?

Perhaps a bigger problem is the way in which we view our available time. Benjamin Franklin famously wrote that 'Time is money',[7] explaining that time that could have been spent profitably working but that was actually used in 'diversion or idleness' cost not only any money spent in that time but also those hours of 'lost' wages. This attitude is reinforced by the way money grows through interest payments, increasing merely through the passage of time and not through any productive work. The fact that many jobs are now paid by the hour, rather than by the day or by yearly salary, encourages the idea that time has intrinsic monetary value. For some professionals, such as lawyers, whose time is measured in 'billable hours' (the time they work that can directly be charged to clients), the tensions this toxic mindset causes are particularly acute. As one journalist summarizes: 'It's a classic, needling lawyer's question: spend two hours at your daughter's soccer game, or bill the time and pocket $1,400?[8]

Time and money are often linked more or less closely, encouraging us either to value time or to count the cost of 'wasted' hours and minutes. Overtime is typically valued at one and a half or double the

> *'Time is money.'*
> *Benjamin Franklin*

regular pay-rate. Taking statutory sick pay, maternity pay and unpaid holiday all carry financial consequences. Penalty clauses, whether on complex building projects or a simple pizza delivery, reinforce the importance of deadlines. TV and radio advertisers pay for time in ten-second blocks (as well as for particular slots of time). Mobile phone companies bill by the minute or second.

Not only do we feel pushed for time, but the blurring of minutes and money means that we may not enjoy our time off so much because we know exactly what it 'costs' us. Even if we do not view time quite so commercially, we still feel the urgency to 'spend' our time wisely and fruitfully.

Biblical time

So what does the Bible have to say about the way we slice up our lives? In a society without accurate clocks, if any, broad divisions and markers of time such as day and night, morning, noon and sundown, stood in place of our strict allocation of hours, minutes and seconds. It is not until the New Testament that even the sense of an 'hour' as a twelfth of the day appears,[9] as in the parable of the vineyard, in which workers are hired first early in the morning, and then at the third, sixth, ninth and finally eleventh hours (Matt. 20.1–16). So it is hardly surprising that our sense of time-related stress is also missing. But what can we infer from a time when time was not, at first glance, taken seriously?

In Psalm 90, Moses acknowledges that time is limited – 'The length of our days is seventy years – or eighty, if we have the strength' – and that we must spend it purposefully (Ps. 90.10–12). The biblical writers understood the need not to waste time. Proverbs repeatedly warns the 'sluggard' of his impending ruin and praises the hard worker. 'Lazy hands make a man poor, but diligent hands bring wealth. He who gathers crops in summer is a wise son, but he who sleeps during harvest is a disgraceful son' (Prov. 10.4–5). Paul warns the Corinthians that time is short and urges them not to become engrossed in the things of the world, because they are only temporary (1 Cor. 7.29–31).[10] He writes to the Ephesians, 'Be very careful, then, how you live – not as unwise but as wise, making the most of every opportunity, because the days are evil' (Eph. 5.15–16). Other translations read, 'redeeming the time, because the days are evil'.

> '*Many people take no care of their money till they come nearly to the end of it, and others do just the same with their time.*'
> *Johann Wolfgang von Goethe, writer and philosopher*

Despite its encouragements to use time wisely and to work hard, the Bible doesn't see work as the ultimate good: economic productivity is not the main purpose of time, as we often assume, whether implicitly or explicitly. Ecclesiastes says that there is a *zᵉmān* ('appointed time') for everything, and an *'ēt* ('appropriate time') for every activity under the sun (3.1). Our days and minds were never supposed to be filled with just one activity. This is reinforced by the fourth commandment: 'Six days shall you labour and do all your work, but the seventh day is a Sabbath to the LORD your God' (Exod. 20.9–10).

Unlike our current culture, in the Bible time was not viewed as the most precious resource we have. In 1 Kings 3, God offers the new king Solomon, 'whatever you want me to give you'. Painfully aware of his inexperience, Solomon asks for wisdom to rule his kingdom. 'The LORD was pleased that Solomon had asked for this. So God said to him, "Since you have asked for this and not for long life or wealth for yourself . . . I will do what you have asked"' (1 Kings 3.5–12).

Wisdom is valued more highly than 'long life or wealth', time or money. Proverbs reiterates this: wisdom 'is more profitable than silver', 'yields better returns than gold' and is 'more precious than rubies' (Prov. 3.13–15). Long life and riches are the fruit of wisdom (v. 16), but not ends to be chased in their own right. One of the major blessings of long life in the Old Testament is family and relationships: Job 'saw his children and their children to the fourth generation' (Job 42.16). Joseph 'lived a hundred and ten years and saw the third generation of Ephraim's children' (Gen. 50.22–23). 'Children's children are a crown to the aged, and parents are the pride of their children' (Prov. 17.6). By contrast, Ecclesiastes 4.7–8 highlights the futile misery of working endlessly for wealth without the blessing of others to enjoy it with you.

Sabbath

The Hebrew calendar marked out God's sovereignty over time by remembering at regular intervals throughout the year his acts in history and his ongoing care for the Israelites: Passover, the Feast of Weeks and the Feast of Tabernacles (Deut. 16.1–17). More festivals were added later to commemorate other significant events.

On a weekly basis, God's sovereignty over time was recognized in the observance of the Sabbath. One day in every seven, everybody had to stop work: 'Six days you shall labour and do all your work, but the seventh day is a Sabbath to the LORD your God. In it you shall not do any work . . .' (Deut. 5.13–14). As one of the Ten Commandments, the Sabbath rest was given the highest importance.

There are many different reasons for placing such a significance on a day of rest – just as there were many different areas of life on which the Sabbath break impacted. Genesis 2.3 reads, 'And God blessed the seventh day and made it holy, because on it he rested from all the work of creating that he had done.' With similar language, Exodus 20.11 suggests that the purpose of the Sabbath is to remember and appreciate this act of creation: 'For in six days the LORD made the heavens and the earth, the sea, and all that is in them, but he rested on the seventh day. Therefore the LORD blessed the Sabbath day and made it holy.'

In Deuteronomy 5.15, God's act of deliverance from slavery in Egypt is emphasized: 'Remember that you were slaves in Egypt and that the LORD your God brought you out of there with a mighty hand and an outstretched arm. Therefore the LORD your God has commanded you to observe the Sabbath day.' As slaves in Egypt, the Israelites did not have the option to rest, and the Sabbath commemorates the Exodus and the freedom from the unending, oppressive work that was part of their history.

Indirectly, there are further clues as to why the Sabbath was – and still is – so important. The prophet Amos made a link between dishonouring the day of rest and injustice when he criticized the traders who were desperate for the Sabbath to end:

Hear this, you who trample the needy and do away with the poor of the land, saying, 'When will the New Moon be over that we may sell grain, and the Sabbath be ended that we may market wheat?' – skimping the measure, boosting the price and cheating with dishonest scales, buying the poor with silver and the needy for a pair of sandals, selling even the sweepings with the wheat. (Amos 8.5–6)

27

To these traders, the Sabbath was not a time of rest and remembrance, but an inconvenience to be endured impatiently as an interruption to their normal routine of making money. It is not a coincidence that these same traders used false measures and dishonest weights, one of the only regulations on free trade in the Old Testament (Deut. 25.13). The Sabbath felt like a chore because they had become obsessed with making money, and a day off got in the way of their commerce. When money becomes more important than any other concern, dishonesty in the pursuit of this objective naturally follows. The question that lies behind Amos's words, and the two versions of the Commandment in Exodus and Deuteronomy, is: 'Who is your God?'

> I already have to work most Saturdays, so Sunday was the one day I got to spend with my whole family. Since I've had to start some shifts on a Sunday, I don't even get that. And it's no good my employer saying I still have a day off in the week – the children are at school then. The only time I get to spend quality time with them any more is in the school holidays.   Sandra, 34

As we move gradually towards a 24/7 society, in which time is money and global markets are never closed, this question is just as relevant. If the economy never sleeps and shops are open for business day and night, every day of the week, when do we get to rest? Along with the divine aspect of the Sabbath comes the human dimension. It is a time to remember who we are and what really matters – to renew and refresh our relationships with God and with each other by purposefully spending time on them, rather than allowing the distractions of the rest of the week to crowd in. It is a time to stop and rest from the things that could easily become idols if we let them.

There is a clear link between long and unsociable work hours, and relationship breakdown and dysfunction, which have enormous personal and financial consequences for individuals, families and society as a whole.[11] Treating this one ring-fenced day of the week as just the same as any other ignores the importance of rest, relationships and other aspects of life that resist material evaluation. Some Christians, such as doctors, will have to work on Sunday, but the shared day off for friends and family reminds us that work and consumption are not our reasons for living.

> '*Industrious races find it a great hardship to be idle: it was a master-stroke of* English *instinct to hallow and begloom* Sunday *to such an extent that the Englishman unconsciously hankers for his week- and work-day again . . .*'
> Friedrich Nietzsche[12]

It is easy to caricature the Sabbath as a day of enforced inactivity, even laziness, rather than as a positive time of rest and refreshment in which we purposefully give time to those aspects of our lives that should be most important. In the New Testament, as in Amos, this was a common misunderstanding of what the Sabbath was really for. Jesus was criticized for doing 'work' on the Sabbath on several occasions, even though this was often healing the sick. The Pharisees had built up volumes of rules and complicated discussions around the Commandments (later recorded in the Talmud), meaning that their intention to honour God by observing the Law in every tiny detail risked becoming cold and legalistic. For example, it was said that making brine (perhaps for curing hides, which was considered work) was forbidden on the Sabbath, but a weaker solution of salt water (perhaps for seasoning food) was permitted. This raised the question of exactly *how much* salt could be added to water before the process constituted 'work'. One school of thought maintained that 'If one put an egg into the water and the egg float (*sic*) it is strong salt water [i.e. brine].'[13] This excessive caution meant that non-urgent healing, for example of injuries that were not life-threatening, was also not permitted (the background to the Pharisees' accusation in Mark 3.1–6).

Keen to avoid such legalistic applications that missed the true purpose of the Sabbath, Jesus carefully qualifies this commandment: 'Then he said to them, "The Sabbath was made for man, not man for the Sabbath. So the Son of Man is Lord even of the Sabbath"' (Mark 2.27–28). The commandment ensured a day in which work did not take precedence over our relationships with God and family; Jesus' words ensure that we are not slaves to rigid divisions of time and that worse outcomes do not arise from our misunderstanding of the commandment itself. 'The Sabbath was made for man': time has been separated and designated for our benefit, not to rule us.

Roots

In understanding how time is important, we also have to grasp the significance of place. If time is the currency of relationships, then where we put down roots – our time in one place – is also crucially important. Our closest relationships are the ones in which we invest time, a process that's far easier if we live in the same community.

In Old Testament Israel, the Law supported family relationships. The land was a gift from God to the Israelites. On their entry into Canaan, it was divided into areas (Josh. 13–19), which remained within the extended family and could not be permanently bought or sold. Every 50 years, every family that had sold or lost their land returned to their ancestral plot (Lev. 25.8–17). Families and wider kinship groups lived in the same area, meaning that every family had access to productive ground and therefore shared economic interests. Further laws around debt aimed to encourage family and clan members to help each other and avoid where possible any family member needing to move away (Lev. 25.35). However, the allotment of land gave each family a strong, shared geographical and religious identity that involved far more than purely financial considerations. When King Ahab tries to purchase Naboth's vineyard, he protests, 'The Lord forbid that I should give you the inheritance of my fathers' (1 Kings 21.3).[14]

Modern life is very different. University leavers rarely settle in their home areas, and people frequently move around for work. As a broad indicator of mobility, there were 1.7 million house sales in the UK in 2006 and 1.6 million in 2007.[15] As the credit crunch bit in 2008, the number dropped to 0.9 million and even further in the initial months of 2009, before stabilizing. Mobility is seen as the price of success – sometimes it's even the reward. But the process of leaving behind a community and established relationships is stressful. New relationships may not have time to flourish, and people are less willing to invest time to make new friends if they know they will be moving again soon. If one partner works in another town, leading to a long daily or even weekly commute, this can lead to stretched, fragmented and shallow relationships. The relational breakdown that often results can drive further mobility and an increasingly individualistic outlook, which leads in turn to even greater breakdown.

Lucinda was a woman waiting for an affair to happen, though she did not realize this for some time. She was in her late thirties, pretty, very lively and intelligent, and was taking a career break to bring up her four children. The trouble was that she felt her husband was taking a break from their marriage to build his career. It was very important for him to climb to the top of his profession. Even his parents said when she complained to them, 'You must try not to make things difficult for him by burdening him with your demands. It's natural he wants to make a success of his career. You should be prepared to take a back seat. And look at the lifestyle you have. What are you complaining about?'

Harry, her husband, was a couple of years older than Lucinda and seemed to share much the same view as his parents. For the past four years of their fifteen-year marriage he had spent more and more time at work, leaving before seven in the morning, and rarely arriving home before ten o'clock at night. He hardly ever called her from work, unless he wanted a lift from the station, or to tell her that he would be having dinner in town with the other guys from work, so she needn't wait up for him.

Lucinda said, 'Matt made me feel interesting, desirable, pretty, and fun to be with. He said all the things I wanted to hear and did all the things I wanted him to do. They were all things I wanted Harry to do and say, but Harry never did. I felt I was at the bottom of Harry's list of priorities, but with Matt I was at the top.'[16]

Important though roots are, Jesus qualifies their significance for family and other long-term relationships. Although these are important, they cannot take priority over the kingdom of God. As Christians, our identity is first and foremost found in the Church and fellowship of believers, and only second in a geographical area. Although Jesus' earthly family was important to him (honouring your parents is one of the Ten Commandments), his first loyalty was to his heavenly father, and travel in the course of his ministry was an intrinsic part of this. 'Jesus replied, "Foxes have holes and birds of the air have nests, but the son of man has nowhere to lay his head"' (Matt. 8.20). It may be necessary for us to weigh the importance of roots against the need to move for God's work; obviously some mobility is required if the Great Commission to reach the ends of the earth with the gospel is to be fulfilled (Matt. 28.19–20).

For all that our loyalty must first be to the kingdom of God, in practice this priority is rarely a factor when it comes to moving.

Mobility can be something we just take for granted, the price of pursuing the jobs and courses we want, to the detriment of the extended family. It's also worth remembering that Jesus stayed at home until he was 30 – as the eldest son, he would have had particular responsibilities to the family. His family mattered deeply to him, and even on the cross one of his last actions was to make arrangements for his mother's support (John 19.26–27).

Time and timeliness

Even a brief study of the Bible shows a radically different approach to time from the one presupposed by modern society. Our culture does its best to squeeze every last second out of the day, to make the most of every moment. We feel cheated if we are not 'spending' our time productively and extracting its maximum value – whether in work, leisure or even sleep.

As a result, we end up counting the time-cost of everything we do, rationing hours and minutes but never producing any more. As Jesus asks in Matthew 6.27, 'Who of you by worrying can add a single hour to his life?' When we think of 'time', it is more often in the context of 'time to' do the next thing than 'time for' someone or something.

> 'Westerners have watches but no time. Africans have time but no watches.'
> *Kenyan saying*

Jesus' approach to time was quite striking. He was always flexible in how he spent his time, working with the crowds and individuals who sought him out at awkward times, at night or when he was in the middle of teaching his disciples. In Mark 5, he let a serious but non-urgent case (a woman who had been sick for 12 years and wasn't in imminent danger of death) interrupt him on his way to an urgent one, eventually arriving 'too late', after the girl had died. He allowed interruptions and used them for God's glory, in this case, of course, by raising the girl. Are there ways in which we can do the same? It can be easy to focus so hard on one area of ministry that we ignore other areas of need.

I used to help my church run a discussion group for people wanting to know more about Christianity. I would help with the catering. It was always frantic. I worked hard, cleared up after the meeting and was always last out of the church, late at night. Barely anyone said 'thank you', or offered to help. I felt taken for granted. I don't know what the others got out of the evening, but I know I became disillusioned with Christians as a result. It's strange that the leaders would work so hard to bring people into the church, when just a few kind words or gestures might have stopped someone else from leaving.

Paul, 28

Timing was also important in the raising of Lazarus, in John 11. 'Jesus loved Martha and her sister and Lazarus. Yet when he heard that Lazarus was sick, he stayed where he was two more days' (John 11.5–6). Jewish belief at the time seems to have been that the soul did not finally leave the corpse until the fourth day, when decomposition started. 'For three days the soul hovers over the body, intending to re-enter it, but as soon as it sees its appearance change, it departs, as it is written, "When his flesh that is on him is distorted, his soul will mourn over him" (Job 14.22).'[17] Some commentators believe that Jesus' delay was to ensure that his onlookers could not claim that Lazarus had a chance of revival anyway: four days meant that he really was completely dead. 'For your sake I am glad I was not there, so that you may believe' (John 11.14).

Often Jesus would spend time with God very early in the day. Right through his ministry he divided his time between teaching large crowds of people and spending it with a small number of the people closest to him, but whatever he did, he always made sure he had plenty of time alone to pray – the 'first fruits' of his time. It's a great challenge to us to use our time the same way, rather than relegate God and our supposedly closest relationships to a few minutes here and there, or the exhausted end of the day.

Meditation

Be very careful, then, how you live – not as unwise but as wise, making the most of every opportunity, because the days are evil. Therefore do not be foolish, but understand what the Lord's will is. (Eph. 5.15–17)

Discussion questions

- What do you consider to be 'work'? Employment – paid work? DIY, cleaning, gardening, and other jobs around the house? Homework/ college work or other study?
- What makes or doesn't make each of these 'work', and why would or wouldn't you want to do them on particular days of the week or at certain times of the day?
- Does God get the 'first fruits' of your time? If not, how might you change this?
- Do you feel that you 'spend' or 'invest' your time?

4

Selling sex

―――――・◆・―――――

A month after my 29th birthday I decided to stop having sex. I'd had plenty of sexual partners (30 or so), a sprinkling of one-night stands, a fair balance between 'making love' and 'just' sex. I had no hang-ups about it – indeed, it was getting better as I got older. I'd had serious boyfriends, and I'd had many more less serious ones whom I'd dated for a few weeks or months. I'd had my requisite lesbian experiments – it's practically a twenty-first-century requirement.

But on the cusp of my thirties I suddenly realized I didn't want to keep racking up the numbers, continuing on the same path I was on. I was over sexual liberation, a feminist doctrine that had gained us the right to enjoy our sexuality, and by extension promiscuity, without repudiation. I felt like dating had become a burlesque comedy where we all pretended we were emotionless and cool – when in actual fact dating was a fruitless, haunting quest for a snatch of intimacy, a warm body, a less-lonely night. Sex had become an obligation, not a choice. I wanted sex to be, quite simply, special again . . .

In the past, I had relied too much on playing the vamp, on trying to 'hook' a boyfriend with my purported sexual prowess. I felt, almost unconsciously, that to be 'worth' something in the cattle-market of dating, I also had to hold a packed résumé of sexual skills – acts so intimate that they are absurdly remote from any form of intimacy, particularly when performed like the quicktime with a relative stranger on date three . . . I realized I'd been unable to separate sex and intimacy. I had, in effect, slept with most of [my last four sexual partners] way before I felt comfortable with the fact, merely because I'd had the resigned attitude that 'I've done it so many times before, why not?' Anonymous[1]

The way we think about love and sex has changed over the last few decades. Some of the cultural shifts might be bad, others are definitely good, but one way or another there's no question that things are very different.

Two of the most famous romance movies of all time, 1942's *Casablanca* and 1997's *Titanic*, illustrate this change well. Admittedly, comparing films doesn't exactly satisfy scientific requirements for proof, but it's hard to argue against millions of cinema-goers when it comes to judging sea changes in popular culture. In both of the films a couple – Rick and Ilsa in *Casablanca*, Jack and Rose in *Titanic* – meet unexpectedly, only to be kept apart at the end by circumstances beyond their control. But although there are some superficial similarities, the two films have striking differences. In *Casablanca* it is Rick's sense of duty, patriotism and love for Ilsa that lead him to allow her to escape danger without him. In *Titanic*, as the film's tagline states, 'Nothing On Earth Could Come Between Them': only death could separate the lovers. In *Casablanca*, the context of Rick's decision is the Second World War, with its millions of casualties and atrocities. In *Titanic*, the love story somehow takes centre stage over the sinking of the ship, which becomes little more than a plot device to separate the lovers, rather than a tragedy in which 1,500 people died. In the later film, as many Christian writers have noted, the love affair takes on a curious, almost spiritual significance. 'He saved me . . . in every way that a person can be saved . . .', says Rose many years later. But 55 years earlier in *Casablanca*, a key line was: 'it doesn't take much to see that the problems of three little people don't amount to a hill of beans in this crazy world'.

Clearly, something happened in between.

Actually, a lot of things have happened. *Casablanca* and *Titanic* are only films, but like most films they reflect the attitudes of the times in which they were made. A quick survey of national statistics gives a clearer overview of some of the changes of the last few decades. In 1960, there were 344,000 marriages in the UK and just 26,000 divorces. Today, there are around 270,000 marriages,[2] 144,000 divorces[3] and 198,500 abortions a year.[4] Homosexual sex was only decriminalized in 1967; in 2006 there were 16,106 civil partnerships, 8,728 in 2007 and 7,169 in 2008. Before the 1960s, living together outside of marriage was rare;[5] now around 2.3 million people are cohabiting in the UK at any given time.

In his landmark book, *Sex and the iWorld*, Dale Kuehne describes these two cultures as the traditional 'tWorld' of the past and individualistic 'iWorld' of the present. Although not all of the changes are unwelcome or negative – and no one is pretending that the 'tWorld' was a perfect place, by any means – there is no denying that the differences are stark.

> Marriage and the extended family were the relational framework of the tWorld. They were so important and constant that whether you lived in the tWorld one hundred years ago or several thousand years ago, your identity and your life were rooted in a well-ordered relational structure . . . In the tWorld *happiness* was deeply connected to the quality of our relationships. If we lived in a good family, a good neighbourhood, and a good city and had good friends, we had most of what we needed to be happy. Human happiness and fulfilment was primarily dependent on the health of this relational matrix. [Within the tWorld,] sexuality was a drive and an appetite that had a function and a purpose . . . rather than an agent of personal or relational fulfilment.[6]

The iWorld marks a dramatic departure from 'tWorld' values:

> We live in a time in which the nature of the way we think about the world and ourselves is changing . . . It is an era in which long-established boundaries are dissolving in the belief that individual moral and relational choice will yield the greatest level of happiness and fulfilment for which we yearn.[7]

Sex and the Bible

In comparison to the iWorld's overwhelming emphasis on personal freedom, the Bible's 'tWorld' teaching on sex seems, unsurprisingly, completely outdated and irrelevant. Genesis describes how God's pattern for marriage at Creation was 'one flesh' (Gen. 2.20–24). This passage and other biblical teaching make it clear that this means one man and one woman in a permanent, faithful relationship.[8] In the New Testament, both Jesus and Paul quote this 'one flesh' Creation passage to make two different but related points. Jesus uses it in an argument against the Pharisees to prove that, although the Old Testament allows divorce, this was a concession to humans' hardness of heart and not God's will – in fact, he argues that divorce and remarriage without just cause is the same as adultery, since if there wasn't a good reason for a divorce then the marriage still stands. 'Therefore what God has joined together, let man not separate' (Matt. 19.6). Sex – 'one flesh' – joins two people permanently in God's sight.

This is not to say that they cannot be separated, only that they should not be, as this is a distortion of the Creation ideal. Paul also argues that sex has permanent consequences. Even if it is a brief or casual relationship, such as a one-night stand or sex with a prostitute, it still has ongoing spiritual and physical significance (1 Cor. 6.12–20). In the Old Testament, this was recognized by laws that required a man to marry a woman he had slept with, or at the very least to provide for her financially if her family refused marriage for some reason (Exod. 22.16–17). (The father's role in deciding reflects the different cultural norms and the fact that he was responsible for her financially until her marriage.) In biblical terms, sex effectively *is* marriage.[9] The Creation pattern in Genesis 2.24, as understood by Jesus and Paul, suggests that the bond created by sex between man and woman should be lifelong and exclusive.

Someone to blame

'I've got a little list / of benefit offenders who I'll soon be rooting out / And who never would be missed . . . Young ladies who get pregnant just to jump the housing list.'
Secretary of State for Social Security, Conservative Party conference, 1992

Over the years many different groups have been targeted as the cause or the worst aspect of society's sexual breakdown. In 1993 under John Major, the Conservatives' Back to Basics campaign placed responsibility for the high cost of social welfare squarely at the feet of single mothers. (At the time, Britain was just emerging from the last recession, so any cuts in public spending were welcome.) Back to Basics was viewed by many as a 'moral crusade' and dropped out of sight after a series of sexual and financial scandals were uncovered within the Conservative party, effectively raising the moral high ground out of their reach. For Christians, various other targets have risen and fallen in popularity from time to time, particularly gay men, abortion and teenage pregnancy. But although different aspects of society's changing sexual landscape might seem significant and have particular consequences, looking at it this way misses the point.

In 2007, Irish traffic police finally caught up with a Polish driver responsible for a one-man crime wave. Prawo Jazdy had racked up dozens of speeding tickets and parking offences, but had never been brought to justice. Every time police stopped him, he gave a different address – he had over 50 identities on file. Eventually an officer realized what had happened. Rather than being the name of a man, Prawo Jazdy – written in large blue letters in the top right-hand corner of every licence-card – is the Polish for 'driving licence'. Every time they had stopped a motorist, officers had looked at the licence and recorded the two most obvious words from the lines of unfamiliar text, assuming that what they were reading was a name. The same knee-jerk reaction is true of sexual morality: although it's easy to latch on to the big 'headline' issues like high divorce rates, abortion and sexually transmitted infections, these are just symptoms of a much deeper problem. They need addressing in and of themselves, but at the same time it's too easy for us to miss the wood for the trees.

The sexual revolution that began in the 1960s saw sexual standards relaxed, as effective contraception became widely available. Although contraception has great benefits in limiting family size and poverty, and in giving the option to wait before having children, the change in values that resulted cannot be overestimated. Alongside the medical and cultural changes of the last 50 years, sex has also come to *mean* something different, and to serve a different purpose, especially in the lives of individuals who look for new relationships. Because a couple *could*, in theory, have sex without pregnancy following sooner or later, the assumption developed that they *should*. With no intrinsic connection between sex and family, with its implications of permanence and responsibility, sexual relationship became more about the couple, and about individual choice. Its meaning has shifted towards more individual and couple-focused benefit, and is increasingly about personal identity – the change that is aptly illustrated by the different roles of love and romance in *Casablanca* and *Titanic*, and countless other popular films.

Sex and consumer choice

Like everything else in our consumer-driven culture, sex risks becoming little more than a commodity or a choice to pursue, to enjoy and then to change when it suits us. Many people upgrade their mobile phones on a yearly basis or even more frequently; a lot of sexual relationships don't even last that long.

Advertising has played on and encouraged the consumerization of sex. Sex is used to sell all kinds of products, from coffee to cars. Even the women in the Scottish Widows adverts have, against statistical probability, all been models who first don the black cloak in their early twenties and hand it on before they are too far into their thirties. When you stop to think about it, the message that lies behind this kind of advertising is pretty blunt: 'buy this brand of deodorant/jeans/chewing gum/pension and you will have more sex' – a sentiment that would obviously be ludicrous if it weren't such an effective advertising technique.

The attractive woman is sitting alone at a table outside a coffee shop, enjoying her drink and keeping half an eye on the steady stream of pedestrians passing by in both directions. They are all men, though this detail doesn't seem as odd as it should for some reason. Tall, short, wiry, muscular, smartly or casually dressed, all nationalities, wealthy, successful, handsome . . . the stream of men flows past, like an endless, moving buffet table.

But suddenly she finds that someone has caught her eye. He's clearly very special, because despite the fact that this is the first time she has met him, it is somehow obvious that this is the beginning of a lifelong romance. She stands up to join him, and they embrace.

So what can it be that she finds so irresistibly attractive? Ok, he's good-looking and well-dressed, but so are all the other . . . ah, of course. His glasses: the only failsafe indicator of the prospects for a long-term romantic relationship. And what an outstanding pair of specs they are. There's absolutely no question of anything other than happily-ever-after with a set of frames like that.

The couple walk away together, surrounded by all the disappointed men who foolishly chose a different brand of eyewear.

But perhaps at a more insidious level, there is a second way in which sex is used in advertising, as well as in TV, film and other media. Rather than just playing on a straightforward biological urge and associating it with the product in question, sex is used as a shorthand for intimacy. The message of many commercials and entertainment shows is that the best kind of relationship is the sexual one, and that if you want to know someone fully and experience true intimacy with them, you must have sex with them.

In a society in which non-sexual intimacy has been damaged by family breakdown, high rates of mobility for work, university and other reasons, and even the consumerization of relationships itself, there can be a great attraction to this kind of quick fix to loneliness – hence the near-ubiquitous romance plot or subplot in film. And, of course, sex and intimacy often do go together, so the association is not an unbelievable one. But the message is often that sex precedes and creates intimacy, rather than arising necessarily within an already stable and intimate relationship.

This is an extremely harmful message, because it places sex and romance above every other kind of relationship, including close friendships and family relationships – which are logically viewed as 'second best'. It tells us that the first question we should ask on meeting someone of the opposite sex is whether they might make a better partner than friend and, if so, that these should be the grounds on which we approach the relationship as it progresses. It also encourages us to sexualize or romanticize existing friendships. Close friendships often do lead to romance and can provide strong foundations – partly because it is easier to get to know someone who isn't just trying to present the best side of themselves because they want to be at their most attractive. However, doing so on the grounds that romance would be a 'better' form of relationship and intimacy, or because our culture is sceptical about the possibility of 'just' friendship between men and women, is putting the cart before the horse. It means assuming that there might be something missing from a close friendship, which could potentially be improved by sex/romance.

If there is one place that should go out of its way to disprove the idea that love equals sex, it must be the Church. Christians have to value friendship as friendship, not as a route to something else. We have to model non-sexual intimacy, and churches must be places where being 'just' friends is fine – where others know that friendships aren't started with another agenda in mind, and where there isn't the assumption that a friendship between two people of the opposite sex is really something 'more'. Married Christians must also model this to people other than their partner, and singles to married friends, albeit with care not to mislead anyone, or cross the line themselves. Jesus didn't exclude himself from striking up friendships with anyone on the grounds of their relationship status.

Sexual 'freedom'

The consumerization of sex comes with more problems than the damage to wider relationship and real intimacy. A society so flooded with sexual content makes certain assumptions about how people should act towards one another. Another critic even explains the decline in topless sunbathing on French beaches as a result of this pressure; whereas feminists once fought for the right to go topless, like men, the sheer quantity of sexual imagery now means that there are, almost by default, expectations on women.

> More and more women came to feel harassed by the 'porno-chic' trend that put nearly-naked women on billboards everywhere. 'Being able' to go topless gradually evolved into feeling obliged to do so, and eventually, the prevailing feminist perspective changed from revelling in a new-found freedom to refusing to give in to the endless pressure to flaunt a 'perfect' body.[10]

In *A Return to Modesty*, Wendy Shalit attacks the culture that has meant that what were once considered sexual freedoms have led to reduced freedom, and increased fear: 'If our culture always expects young women to be playing with their sexual power, always at the ready for the advances of anyone, this means they never have the right to say "no".'[11]

In a society in which sex has become consumerized and commercialized, used to advertise just about everything under the sun, it's inevitable that sex itself comes to be for sale. Prostitution is nothing new; it is found in almost every culture in history. But like casual sex, abortion, divorce and adultery, over recent years our cultural attitudes towards it have shifted. Prostitution is seen increasingly in individualistic terms of personal freedom, meaning the prostitute's right to sell sex, and the purchaser's right to buy it. The problem is that – apart from reinforcing the existing cultural mentality – placing such a high value on the rights of the individual and reducing sex to an economic transaction results in far worse injustice. The 'Women Not For Sale' report in 2008 found that 75 per cent of local newspapers carried adverts for prostitutes, and that such adverts could be found in every area of the UK. 'Next to the ads where it says skip hire and lost pets you'll find "fresh girls in every week", "girls age 18 to 24 from Africa, from South East Asia". Within these ads are girls who've been trafficked into modern day slavery.'[12] For the newspapers, such adverts bring in revenue, but their market-driven decision overlooks the human suffering involved.

While human trafficking represents the extreme end of our society's consumerization of sex, 'selling' sex, whether literally or figuratively, is harmful to wider relationships. In every form of sexual expression outside of marriage, there is a separation of sex from the Creation ideal of lifelong, heterosexual, monogamous and exclusive relationship.[13] For the Christian, Paul warns that there is also the question of how it disrupts our relationship with God:

> Do you not know that your body is a temple of the Holy Spirit, who is in you, whom you have received from God? You are not your own; you were bought at a price. Therefore honour God with your body. (1 Cor. 6.19–20)

Consenting adults?

> '*I think most adults would say that whatever in that spectrum somebody does, provided it doesn't hurt anybody, provided it's consensual, provided it's among adults, provided it's in private, it concerns nobody but the people doing it.*'
> Max Mosley, former president of FIA, Formula One's governing body

Hand in hand with the consumerization of sex goes the mantra: 'sex between consenting adults doesn't harm anyone else'. This is really just a convenient justification for sexual acts that might once have been viewed as immoral, but that now are considered normal and natural and that there are apparently no good reasons to avoid. The 'consenting adults' concept has been repeated so many times that it has become a cultural gold-standard that few people even think of questioning. In reality, this widely held assumption is a subtle – and invalid – combination of two different principles.

The first is that sex between consenting adults is *legal*, an idea that lies behind current sexual offences legislation.[14] For example, adultery was effectively decriminalized as long ago as the mid eighteenth century. The second is that behaviour that hurts no one else is *morally valid* – a form of the 'Golden Rule' present in almost every religion, including Christianity: 'So in everything, do to others what you would have them do to you, for this sums up the Law and the Prophets' (Matt. 7.12). Somehow we have confused 'legal' with 'moral' and have turned a blind eye to the fact that it is entirely possible for other people to be hurt by sex between 'consenting adults'. With only a little examination the validity of this convenient fusion of principles can be shown to be entirely false.

> '*The twenty-first century's emphasis on unbridled pleasing of the sexual Self too easily obscures the inevitable, tragic consequences of such actions. While it may be more acceptable and easier to see the consequences to the Self, it is not always so acceptable or easy to see the consequences to others.*'
> Sharon Willmer, Developmental Psychologist,
> University of California[15]

The idea that no one other than the direct participants is impacted by a sexual act is a convenient lie. In reality, individuals' lives, families and our entire society are shaped by sexual choices. The impact is most obvious and hardest to deny where an adulterous affair occurs, or in cases of divorce or separation where there are children involved, but is by no means limited to these. As studies repeatedly show, family breakdown is a key factor in poverty, crime, addiction, low educational achievement and reduced life expectancy.[16] Sex even affects later partners; living together before marriage, having a previous cohabitation with someone else, having divorced parents and having a child outside of marriage first are all specific risk factors for divorce.[17] Sexual relationships and couple break-ups affect the extended family, friendship groups, business and professional relationships and wider society.

> In one case known to me, the head teacher of a school was sleeping with the deputy head. When they broke up acrimoniously, it caused huge problems in the school as other teachers took different sides. The quality of teaching was badly affected as a result. Who knows how many children's education suffered thanks to this supposedly 'private' affair between consenting adults?   Anon.[18]

In terms of public spending – and therefore the cost to all of us as taxpayers – the effects of sexual liberty and relationship breakdown are enormous. The direct cost of family breakdown, including tax credits and benefits, housing needs, healthcare, civil and criminal justice and education impacts, has been calculated as at least £37 billion, or over £1,200 per taxpayer each year.[19] The wider costs to the economy in terms of stress and lost work hours could total up to twice as much again.[20] But relationship breakdown is about far more than money, and its consequences are far wider-reaching. For example, every year, 150,000 children in the UK will see their parents separate – enough to fill Old Trafford twice over. Around three million children live with a single parent, equivalent to the entire population of Inner London. These children are, on average, at greater risk of poverty, health, educational and behavioural problems.

When we say that sex between consenting adults harms no one else, we do not mean it. What we really mean is that our personal freedoms are so important that it is worth hurting other people in the course of pursuing them – even people who are not involved in the relationship at all. We mean that this 'collateral damage' is a worthwhile price to pay for doing what we want. This is despite the fact that our whole system of morality is supposedly built on the 'harm principle' – that the only legitimate grounds for limiting personal liberty is to prevent harm to other people.[21] Our approach to sexual morality suggests that personal liberty trumps all other considerations.

Biblical sexual ethics

The Bible provides a radically different way of looking at sex. Our society's assumption is that sex that takes place between consenting adults in private affects no one else – one of the reasons that the Bible's penalties for sexual behaviour outside of marriage seem so extreme and unfair. However, the Bible's concern for right relationships in every area of life suggests that these laws are not arbitrary commands but reflect a desire to avoid some forms of harm – whether to individuals, to families, communities, or to the nation as a whole.[22]

The Bible doesn't see society in terms of a collection of individuals, all going about their personal business as they see fit so long as their behaviour doesn't hurt anyone else. It takes a broader view than the one that results from emphasizing 'individual freedoms'. Instead, 'individual ethics are "community shaped"'.[23]

> It says, here is the kind of society the Lord God wants. This God's desire is for a holy people, a redeemed community, a model society through whom God can display a prototype of the new humanity whom he intends to create. God wants a community that will reflect God's own character and priorities, especially marked by justice and compassion. Now if *that* is the kind of society God wants, *this* is the kind of person you must be if you belong to it.[24]

As Christians, we need a better outlook than the literally self-centred starting point of individual freedom. This applies to every area of life, but is particularly important in our sexual relationships, since it is the area that has been most affected by our culture's emphasis on personal liberty above care for the whole community. The 'consenting adults' viewpoint has even filtered through to many churches. In some ways, it is understandable. After all, the harm principle makes sense to Christians. Jesus himself said, 'Do to others as you would have them do to you' (Luke 6.31) – or to put it another way, it only counts as 'sin' if there is harm to another person, or offence against God. The problem is that we have too narrow a definition of harm.

The divine imprint

Genesis 1.26–27 reads, 'Then God said, "Let us make man in our image, in our likeness..."... male and female he created them.' Although it is not entirely clear how this works out from this passage alone, it seems that humanity's division into male and female somehow reflects the nature of God in the Trinity. In Ephesians 5.29–32, Paul writes that the marriage relationship reflects Christ's relationship with the Church. Viewed in those terms, a sexual relationship is suddenly far more than a private matter between two people.

That means changing the way we think about sex and marriage. It means recognizing the importance of faithfulness, which is a fundamental characteristic of God's relationship with his people. It also means putting sex in its rightful context – both in terms of the relationships themselves and in terms of our culture as a whole. In 1 Corinthians, chapters 6 and 7, Paul writes to two different groups of Christians whose misunderstanding of their new faith (perhaps under the influence of pagan philosophy) has led them to make mistakes about sex. The first group, in 1 Corinthians 6.12–20, believe that 'everything is permissible for me' – that, like the food they eat, sex has no wider significance for them. As a result, they have been going to prostitutes, thinking it makes no difference to their relationships with God or each other. The second group, in 1 Corinthians 7.1–7, believe that sex is always wrong, even within marriage. They have given it too much importance and influence over their lives, and some are falling into sin as a result.

The first Corinthian group has a direct parallel in our sexually consumerized culture: the mentality that sex is of no wider significance, and so it doesn't matter if people have one-night stands or brief relationships, or if adverts use it as a gimmick to sell things people wouldn't otherwise buy. The second Corinthian group, who try to avoid sex altogether because they think it's always wrong, don't have a direct parallel today – at least, not a common one. However, there is a similar tendency to give sex an unwarranted significance over our lives in the way it's used to symbolize intimacy, making it not inherently bad but overly important – the mentality that a sexual relationship is the best or only kind of relationship worth having.

Paul's first letter to the Corinthians called on its original readers to avoid two common mistakes about sex in their culture. As Christians today, we also have to be aware of the way our most deeply held and easily assumed values can conflict with our faith, and why. God did not create sex to be trivialized, but neither does he intend it to be the thing that defines our lives above everything else. God created us for relationship with him and each other. Although sex is important, it is only one aspect of that broader picture. That has implications for the way we treat each other in church and in our friendships and other relationships. Churches often draw unhelpful lines between 'singles' and 'marrieds', sometimes in the way they mix after the service or outside church, or even in the way marriage is used in sermon illustrations. In larger churches this might also occur where they are divided into home groups or other groups. Fostering right relationships of all kinds, and creating strong, outward-looking communities in our churches, is one way Christians can counter the isolating loneliness and lack of intimacy in our wider culture, for which the search for sex often acts like a sticking-plaster. Where the Church gets this kind of relational community right, it can be a great attraction to non-Christians. Conversely, when we get it wrong and seem unwelcoming, it can be highly off-putting.

Ultimately, Christians need to think about others before themselves. This principle is easier to put into practice when we are dealing with the way we shop, the way we treat the environment and how we invest our money. But somehow, it's enormously challenging and radically countercultural to apply it to the way we think about sex.

Meditation

> Do you not know that your body is a temple of the Holy Spirit, who is in you, whom you have received from God? You are not your own; you were bought at a price. Therefore honour God with your body.   (1 Cor. 6.19–20)

Discussion questions

- C. S. Lewis talks about the 'four loves'[25] – family affection; friendship; 'eros' or romantic love; and 'agape', unconditional love or Christian charity. How should we approach relationships of each type in church?

- Is your church somewhere that models intimacy of all types well – especially non-romantic intimacy? How and why is this the case?
- How could your church and any groups within it do more to be a welcoming, inclusive and intimate community?

5

Just shopping

———————•◦●◦•———————

Consumers are being overwhelmed by too much choice as they battle through daily dilemmas of what to wear, eat, buy or watch, a survey suggests. Day-to-day decisions – such as what shampoo to use, or what mobile phone to buy – are causing unnecessary stress. Many supermarkets have around 40,000 products on sale; it is thought there are around 18 types of organic cheese, 600 kinds of coffee and more than 400 brands of shampoo.

Our research shows that consumers are finding their own solutions to cope with this increasing burden of choice. Choosing well-known and trusted brands is one, but some people are starting to employ less obvious strategies, like buying only organic products or shopping only on a Friday when the supermarket shelves are less full. As consumer choice grows, consumers are feeling overwhelmed and it is starting to have a negative effect on lives.[1]

'Paralysis by analysis' is the phenomenon that, as the number of choices increases, so does the time and effort taken to evaluate them, as does the likelihood that the final decision will be unsatisfactory because there's a growing suspicion that a better solution must exist – somewhere. Walk into almost any shop today and you're walking into a labyrinth of options. All of them are apparently beneficial to someone or something but, inevitably, none are perfect, and choosing one good cause means neglecting another. Indeed, the decision-making process begins before you even reach the shop (assuming you even leave your computer to do your shopping). Do you go for the convenience and choice of a big supermarket, or support a small local business? And when you get there, do you choose the Fairtrade-labelled foreign product, or something that is in season in the UK? Do you buy Organic from abroad, or a locally grown non-organic version that avoids the food miles? Assuming principles are more important than quality, where do you draw the line? Is it worth paying a little extra, or saving the money and giving the difference to a charity or initiative that you, not the shop management, have chosen? Most of all, does your decision result in a real improvement to people's lives, or is the biggest difference merely the one it makes to your conscience?

> 'That the poor are invisible is one of the most important things about them. They are not simply neglected and forgotten as in the old rhetoric of reform; what is much worse, they are not seen.'
> Michael Harrington, writer and political activist

Isaiah's words, to 'spend ourselves on behalf of the hungry and satisfy the needs of the oppressed' (58.10), are an acute reminder that we, in the West, live lives of comfort and privilege compared to many of those on whom we rely for our food and luxury goods. The relative success of Fairtrade[2] and other similar schemes demonstrates that many consumers are keen to make a difference and will do so voluntarily if they have the chance. The problem is that, with so many alternatives, conflicting information and even misdirection, many people are uncertain where to put their money to make the biggest impact.

When good is the enemy of the best

In Mark 7.10–12, Jesus criticizes the Pharisees who held their own law above that of Moses and, by giving to the Temple, denied a better cause.

> For Moses said, 'Honour your father and your mother,' and, 'Anyone who curses his father or mother must be put to death.' But you say that if a man says to his father or mother: 'Whatever help you might otherwise have received from me is Corban' (that is, a gift devoted to God), then you no longer let him do anything for his father or mother.

Both giving to charity and supporting their parents were good choices, but Jesus argued that the former should not be done at the expense of the latter.

While we might not see our 'charitable' purchasing choices in terms of such direct harm, it remains true that a seemingly good decision can distract us from a better one – particularly when there are so many options available. Is it really worth buying organic blueberries if the trade-off is a high carbon footprint because they have been air-freighted to the UK from the other side of the world? Or does our loyalty to a particular quality overlook something else, perhaps more fundamental?

The range of terms – organic, Fairtrade, GM-free, British – can encourage us to abdicate our responsibility as informed consumers by reducing the issue to a single, often misleading label. For example, less intensive farming methods, the availability of natural feed (grass) and high use of renewable power means that New Zealand lamb is actually up to four times more environmentally friendly in terms of carbon emissions than UK-produced lamb: buying local in this instance can be more harmful to the planet than the alternative.[3] To take a slightly different example, many customers are happy to pay a little more for a pack of Fairtrade-certified coffee at the supermarket.[4] However, of this extra, only about 10 per cent ultimately benefits the producer. The rest goes to the supplier and to help Fairtrade promote their own brand.[5] Of course, 10 per cent is a start, but this seems an inefficient way to make a difference.

> '*We don't have time to go to the PTA meeting or write a letter to the editor. Half our nation doesn't have time to vote. But we all eat, and that means most of us shop. So if the act of shopping and the act of consumption can become an act of reaching out, that is a powerful thing.*'   Paul Rice, CEO of TransFair USA

As consumers, if we are serious about making a difference, we need to be prepared to look at the issues that lie behind food production. Making good choices will involve our time as well as our money. There might be occasions when the best answer is not to buy one or other product at all, but to address the problem they represent in a different way. Most of all, we need to ask ourselves what it is we are really trying to achieve by buying (or not buying) something – beyond paying for a convenient and simplistic label to satisfy our consciences. Inevitably, the issues are rarely the one-dimensional caricature that such a rubber-stamp approach suggests. A few of the different labels and their associated problems are examined below (and Appendix 2 looks more closely at Fairtrade as an example of how complex the problems can be).

Fair trade

The terms 'fair trade' or 'fairly traded' (as distinct from just the Fairtrade brand popularly associated with them) express a broad range of principles employed to address global poverty, perhaps most fundamentally by paying fair prices for goods:

> Fair Trade is a trading partnership, based on dialogue, transparency and respect, which seeks greater equity in international trade. It contributes to sustainable development by offering better trading conditions to, and securing the rights of, marginalized producers and workers – especially in the [global] South. Fair Trade organizations (backed by consumers) are engaged actively in supporting producers, awareness-raising and in campaigning for changes in the rules and practices of conventional international trade ... All involved in Fair Trade accept that it has to include: paying fair prices to producers which reflect the true cost of production, supporting producer organizations in their social and environmental projects, promoting gender equality in pay and working conditions, advising on product development to increase access to markets, committing to long-term relationships to provide stability and security and campaigning to highlight the unequal system of world trade which places profit above human rights and threatens our environment.   ('FINE' criteria)[6]

You can't keep all your eggs in the same basket, so we try many things in Kenya. I tried tea. When I was working for the Kenya Tea Development Agency, buyers asked for Fairtrade. It wasn't easy to become certified, but I saw it was the best way out for our people.

There was a huge impact on the first communities to work with Fairtrade. They were poor communities; they did not have water, dispensaries or schools close to them. The money they got from tea was used for food and clothes, but now they also get a premium that they can use to improve their social living. So far they have set up impressive schools and daycare centres, dispensaries, maternity units, water systems, bridges and roads.

Africa does not need aid; we need to participate in a fairer trading system. Teach us how to fish – do not just give us the fish. You see, the farmer receives just 5 per cent of the wealth in tea. When the consumer pays more for Fairtrade tea, this extra money goes to the farmer and improves lives. But if the whole value chain was made fairer, Africa would be lifted out of poverty.[7]

Julius, retired tea producer

Bananas are currently the best-selling Fairtrade product in the UK – £185 million of over £700 million total Fairtrade sales in 2008 – representing over a quarter of all bananas sold.[8] Coffee is not far behind, with £137 million of Fairtrade sales in 2008.[9] Although the term 'fair trade' spans a broad range of products, much of the discussion below and elsewhere surrounds, or is well illustrated by, the coffee trade.

Trading fairly does not (just) mean Fairtrade

The Fairtrade certification or brand is the most common and well-recognized example of the fair-trade values described above. However, ways to trade fairly are not limited to products that bear the Fairtrade certification. One implication of the name is that other products represent unfair trade by default. While Fairtrade has made great advances in stimulating awareness of trade issues, in some ways the very strength of the Fairtrade brand is problematic in that it encourages us to ignore alternatives. Buying Fairtrade makes a difference to the lives of producers and their families, as the story above shows. But it is not necessarily the best and certainly not the only way to do so.

> 'Fair trade is a very macro term. Fair trade can encompass many things that a Fairtrade certified product can have. But the product isn't certified. It's like going to your local farmers market and buying from a local farmer who you know grows organic produce. But they just haven't spent the money to get the official certification.'
> Nicole Chettero, spokeswoman for TransFair USA[10]

At the end of 2009, UK food labelling guidelines changed to specify whether food imported from the West Bank and other parts of the Palestinian territories was produced by Palestinians or by farmers from Israeli settlements.[11] Much of the surrounding debate centred on the possibility that consumers would use the information to boycott Israeli-grown food, on the grounds that the settlements contravene international resolutions. But one telling (and presumably by no means isolated) response was, 'I don't think it will make any difference whatsoever ... I'd be more interested if it was Fairtrade or not.'[12] Faced with the issues of illegal settlements, theft of land, destruction of property, control of water supplies, military oppression, restriction of movement and obstruction of access to facilities such as healthcare, employment and education, the response was to look for a particular logo – and one that, in the context of West Bank produce, is completely irrelevant.

It comes as a surprise to some people that there are alternatives to Fairtrade. The Fairtrade Foundation is the only *independent* certifier of ethically traded products in the UK.[13] However, companies have set up fair-trading programmes of their own. These inevitably do something different from the Fairtrade brand, either in the degree of 'fairness' they offer, in their specific emphases, or simply in the fact that they do not require a time-consuming and costly certification process at the producer's expense.

For example, Starbucks employs the Coffee and Farmer Equity scheme (CAFE), which is independently verified by Conservation International and builds long-term relationships with producers, who supply Starbucks directly (not via the commodity markets) with high-quality coffee beans. In response to public pressure, Starbucks now purchases large amounts of Fairtrade coffee.

As an illustration of some of the problems of perception around Fairtrade, at the time of writing a 'tall' mug of Fairtrade filter coffee at Starbucks costs the same as one of their regular coffee. But compare also the prices paid by Starbucks to those paid by Fairtrade: as of June 2008, Fairtrade has paid $1.25 per pound for its beans, plus a $0.10 social premium for healthcare and education projects.[14] In contrast, in 2008 Starbucks paid an average of $1.48 per pound for its coffee ($1.49 including third-party certified coffees such as Fairtrade). In an example of a contract from one of their top three coffee origins, Finca El Hato in Guatemala, Starbucks pays $1.42 per pound, of which at least $1.32 goes direct to the farmer. A $0.05 bonus was added as a strategic supplier bonus when the supplier reached particular social and environmental standards.[15] So it appears that buying Fairtrade in this instance means that Starbucks makes a greater profit by selling what some would argue is poorer quality coffee, while less money goes to the producer, for no other reason than that the customer thinks they are doing a good deed.

Range of options

The range of 'ethical alternatives' on the market may be surprising to some readers. Often they will have a particular emphasis – whether on the environment, providing a fair wage, improving quality (thereby enabling producers to demand a higher price without artificially fixing one) or building hospitals and schools. Below is just a small selection of these – the list is not intended to be exhaustive, so look out for other options too.

Coffee

- Good African Coffee (www.goodafrican.com) seeks to help growers through trade, not charity. It trains groups of farmers and shares 50 per cent of profits with growers and their communities. The coffee is sold in supermarkets across the UK.
- Ethical Addictions (www.eacoffee.co.uk) is a Christian-based business that pays more than the minimum price Fairtrade guarantees its producers, runs a transparent business, and gives 11 per cent of profits plus a further $150 per tonne of coffee to African charities involved in social projects, including healthcare, farming training for AIDS orphans and sustainable power plants. Its coffee is available in small shops around the UK but is most easily purchased online.
- Union Hand Roasted (www.unionroasted.com) helps small farmer communities to produce high-quality coffee, paying above Fairtrade prices, improving production methods and income and contributing to social development. Its Rwanda and Ethiopia coffee is stocked by Sainsbury's and Waitrose, and its complete range is available in other independent retailers.
- US-based Café Britt (www.cafebritt.com) pays 'above-market prices to growers who consistently produce outstanding crops', establishes long-term relationships with suppliers, and roasts coffee where it is produced, meaning that these countries (Costa Rica and Peru) can 'export the finished product with all its value added in the country of origin'.
- Starbucks pays above-market prices, often purchasing directly from farms and co-operatives, in addition to being the largest seller of Fairtrade coffee in the world.

- Kingdom Coffee (www.kingdomcoffee.co.uk) is a Christian company that reinvests profit from tea and coffee sales in the countries where it is grown, in social and environmental projects.[16]

Other products

- The Rainforest Alliance (www.rainforest-alliance.org) supports biodiversity and promotes sustainable livelihoods for workers, including basic housing and sanitation. Rather than guaranteeing farmers a minimum price, it provides training to improve quality, thereby enabling producers to demand higher rates. However, only 30 per cent of a container's contents need to be Rainforest Alliance-approved to receive the seal.
- The Waitrose Foundation (www.waitrose.com/food/originofourfood/foundation.aspx) supports fruit producers in South Africa with education, skills and training projects.
- Stop the Traffik's 'Good Chocolate Guide'[17] lists ethical sources for chocolate lovers, including Green & Black's.
- Equitrade (www.equitrade.org) seeks to add value to exports such as chocolate for the producing country by processing crops rather than exporting them as raw materials.
- The Assured Food Standards' Red Tractor mark guarantees the interests of groups such as the National Farmers' Union, the Meat and Livestock Commission, and Dairy UK.
- Kuyichi create fashionable clothing from sustainable and recycled materials.
- Spirit of Nature and similar eco-companies sell organic everyday goods for the home, promoting sustainable and socially aware farming methods.

Further ways to engage

Microfinance charities offer small-scale loans to individuals and families in low-income countries, who are not deemed economically viable for larger financial institutions. The availability of credit means they are able to start small businesses to escape poverty: the model of 'trade, not aid'.

- Kiva (www.kiva.org) connects individuals directly to appropriate entrepreneurs in low-income countries, enabling them to finance a specific project. Loans are usually repaid over the course of 6–12 months.

- Five Talents (www.fivetalents.org.uk) runs microfinance programmes in Africa, Central and South America and Asia, usually with the help of the local Anglican Church. Loans are repaid over six months and groups can request subsequent larger loans as their businesses expand.
- Shared Interest (www.shared-interest.com) is a co-operative lending society offering short- and long-term loans to fair-trade producers working with handicrafts or in food production.
- The Trade Justice Movement (www.tjm.org.uk) campaigns to end the unjust rules in international trade that profit big businesses at the expense of poorer countries.

Local

The idea of locally produced goods seems like a winner to most people – and so it can be. Fruit and vegetables that are grown close to the retail outlet should in theory have a significantly lower carbon footprint than those from further afield because they do not require large amounts of fossil fuels to be burnt in the course of their transport. Also, buying local in farmers' markets creates a relationship and helps to cement a community. In terms of carbon footprint, even produce grown in the far corners of the UK ought to be better than its equivalent from the other side of the world – although this is not always the case, as in the example of New Zealand lamb noted above.

However, we cannot assume that a 'local' label is a solution to all the ills in the production chain. While it can be a useful part of our decision making, to reduce that process to a single word risks washing our hands of the wider issues in the interests of keeping our consciences clear. We need a more nuanced and complete approach if our choices are to result in anything more than this.

Total production factors

The description 'local' only refers to the distance between the producer and the shop. So it's accurate as far as it goes: your food was indeed grown or raised close by. The problem is that this label does not take into account all the other factors that come into play between a seed being planted or a chick hatching, and you enjoying your Sunday lunch at home. The 'food miles' of simply transporting the food from the farm to the outlet represents a tiny fraction of the total carbon cost.

One of the most obvious of these factors is the time of year. Buying British may be a good idea when fruit and vegetables are in season, but if they've been kept in refrigerated storage for months, or have been grown in heated greenhouses over the winter, any carbon benefits over foreign imports will be severely reduced or entirely wiped out, and it often becomes more environmentally friendly to buy produce from abroad.[18] We also have to take into account the carbon cost of fertilizer and feed – a significant part of the reason why New Zealand lamb is generally greener than UK-reared lamb.

Another problem involves the route that food has taken to arrive at the shop – which, chances are, was not as-the-crow-flies. Meat that is marketed as local was probably slaughtered off-site. Because big supermarkets have a tendency towards centralization, the number of abattoirs is declining, leading to a few large ones spread across the country. It doesn't help that each supermarket uses its own abattoirs, rather than the nearest available local one. The meat is then shipped somewhere else for processing and packaging. In 2007, Tesco sold 'local' chicken in northeast Scotland that had actually travelled 499 miles to a packaging plant in Essex, and back again.[19] For that matter, how far do the supermarket's employees travel each day before they start work at the abattoir or packaging plant?

Not least, we need to consider our own part in the chain of events by which we bring food to our homes. Many of us drive to the supermarket to buy a relatively small quantity of food – a highly inefficient way to use fossil fuels. Buying in bulk or making different choices about transport can make as much difference as which goods we purchase in the first place. Our choice of how to cook them and dispose of any waste and packaging is also part of our responsibility: the UK produces 6.7 million tonnes of food waste per year, over 100 kg per person.[20]

Local food vs. global poverty?

Arguments about locally sourced food, food miles and total carbon costs are complicated by the tension between caring for the environment and supporting producers at home or abroad. We may wish to buy British food for environmental reasons, or to support a local business, but many people in low-income countries depend on exports to Britain to survive.

Analysis of total carbon costs suggests that we cannot simply discount these countries on environmental grounds. In fact food produced by the very poorest farmers in low-income countries is likely to have the lowest carbon cost, because there is little mechanization, low energy use, and natural sources of crop nutrients are used. Roses grown in Kenya and flown to the UK typically have only a sixth of the total carbon footprint of Dutch imports. Beans imported from Kenya and Uganda – especially when it's winter in the UK – are also better options than greenhouse-produced versions from Britain. Some retailers have even begun to put an 'air-freight' sticker on such imports to 'warn' consumers of the food miles involved, which amounts to a distortion of the true picture.

At other times there just doesn't seem to be a best option. Targeted shopping may not be the best way to make a difference. Instead, microfinance initiatives or involvement with charities offering training and development give us a way to help directly those farmers who don't currently have another way of making a living.

Organic and GM-free

Organic food is another attraction for the environmental and health-conscious consumer: surely it's better to eat meat that hasn't been raised with the assistance of antibiotics, fruit that hasn't been sprayed with chemicals, and vegetables that haven't been genetically modified?

Pros and cons

There are, as ever, two sides to this debate. There are critics of organic farming who believe that the lower yields it may entail would swallow up any remaining rainforest as the world tries to find enough land to feed its population without 'modern' agriculture; equally, there are those who say that the problem is not the global production of food but its distribution; that organic yields are just as high because the same land is often used for several crops; and that farmers in low-income countries can never hope to feed themselves if they rely on monocultures, mechanization and petrochemical fertilizers. It seems like a good idea, but we still have to ask what it is that we are ultimately trying to achieve.

Scripture requires us to care for the earth: the land is an inheritance for future generations, whose welfare depends on our present stewardship of it. God gave the first man and woman the task of tending the Garden of Eden (Gen. 2.15–18), and the legislation in Leviticus chapter 25 ensured that the land had rest – 'a Sabbath to the LORD' every seventh year – and that each family returned to their allotted inheritance of land every 50 years (the Jubilee year – see Chapter 1). Both the land itself was cared for by designating a regular year in which it lay fallow, and the human significance of land ownership addressed by making sure that families had a long-term source of provision.

Caring for the land is therefore fundamental. Finding a scriptural mandate specifically for *organic* farming is harder. Jesus summarized the Law in terms of love for God and love for one's neighbour. Is buying organic food an expression of 'love'?

It's interesting to look a little more closely at our assumptions of what lies underneath the 'organic' label. 'Organic' does not signify one single quality or process, rather it's a value that spans a number of different requirements. For example, antibiotics are commonly used in poultry farming to prevent infection and encourage growth, and birds farmed using these methods don't qualify as organic. But antibiotics are not in themselves bad; most of us would not think twice about taking antibiotics to cure a serious illness. It is their overuse or misuse, or lack of transparency about their use, that makes us uncomfortable. As a result of this antibiotic policy, some organic meat can contain far more harmful bacteria and parasites – salmonella, toxoplasma and trichinella – than meat from conventionally reared animals.[21]

Not all chemicals are bad

If we are looking for food that is 'better for us', we need to take this into account. When we avoid GM food, what is it we are implicitly objecting to? It's probably not the genetic manipulation of 'natural' strains of plants and breeds of animals, which has been going on since time immemorial: with God's blessing, Jacob was apparently successful in some form of selective breeding programme at his uncle Laban's expense (Gen. 30.25–43). Our concern is more likely to be that some extreme form of genetic modification will prove harmful or irreversible, or the idea that we are 'playing God'.[22]

Use of high-yield hybrid varieties of wheat and rice, as well as the adoption of artificial fertilizers, irrigation and other modern Western farming methods, contributed to India's Green Revolution in the

1960s and 1970s. The Green Revolution has halved the proportion of the population in absolute poverty (lacking necessary food, clothing and shelter) and turned the country into a net exporter of grain. While GM crops have not yet proved to be a magic bullet, and cannot be a complete solution, if they provide viable options for feeding the world's increasing population through higher yields, lower water requirements and improved resistance to pests, then there remains to be found a convincing argument for discontinuing research, albeit such research should be accompanied by strict controls. The patenting issues that lock producers into punitive charges for using the crops year after year also need addressing. But issues of justice and regulation – while not insignificant – do not mean the technology itself is intrinsically harmful.

Although concern for the land and God's creation is present in Scripture, 'all the Law and the Prophets' rest on just two commandments: love for God and for neighbour (Matt. 22.34–40). Care for the environment is a part of both love for God and love for neighbour, but Jesus does not summarize the Law in terms of the environment – only in terms of our relationships. It is too easy to see protection of 'the environment' as a goal in its own right – a mindset that risks turning us into idolaters, or at least environmentalists over and above Christians.

Balanced thinking

That extremes are dangerous is beyond question. Too much use of fertilizer destroys soil quality and pollutes water courses; careless use of pesticides damages biodiversity and disrupts local ecosystems; overuse of antibiotics fosters drug-resistance; the widespread adoption of GM could have long-term risks that have yet to be identified. All this must be weighed against the biblical concern of care for the land; but equally clearly, fertilizers, pesticides, antibiotics and GM can have great benefits when used carefully.

A carrot that has been grown with the assistance of artificial fertilizer is a world apart from a genetically modified and pumped-full-of-hormones 'Frankenstein' cow, but the lack of an 'organic' label puts them on a par with each other as far as the buyer is concerned. Similarly, the organic label does not necessarily guarantee care for the land or people if the product has been grown on former rainforest, if its production involves exploitative labour practices or if the end product has been air-freighted across the world. On the other hand, a product may be grown organically – or be perfectly healthy for us and the environment – but lack the formal certification, which can cost from £250–£600 a year, after a long and often complicated and expensive conversion process to organic farming.

Perhaps the biggest problem is that we, as consumers, are not given enough information to assure our peace of mind – or we do not have the time or expertise to understand the vast amount of data involved. As such, 'organic' can be a convenient way of refusing to engage with those issues, substituting recognizing a label for digesting an enormous volume of information in making the decision whether to eat something or not.

Like 'Fairtrade' and 'local', the 'organic' certification can reduce the issues behind our purchasing choices to this recognition of a single label, encouraging us to wash our hands of the real concerns in the interests of easy decision. As such, it risks becoming a catch-all solution to our many worries – real, vague or imagined – about the food we eat. We need to remember that, while care for the land is a biblical and important concern, Jesus summarized our faith in terms of love for God and each other. The 'organic' label may provide one antidote to overintensive farming, but caring for the land and other people is not dependent on, or inseparable from, organic farming.

The global picture

Recently, a combination of factors has highlighted the myth of the individualistic consumer. Within the space of a few months, we suddenly had proof that we can't live our lives as we choose without consequences to ourselves or other people. The credit crunch has shown us that we cannot borrow indiscriminately without, as one critic put it, the toxic chickens eventually coming home to roost. The cost of oil rose to its highest level ever in July 2008, forcing many people to restrict the travel and lifestyles they had enjoyed. At the same time, food prices soared, prompting questions about what we can afford to eat that most had taken for granted. It is likely that we are moving into a time of prolonged global food shortages. Food prices have risen sharply and are expected to continue rising in the long run, as competition for limited resources grows. How do we see the issues above in the light of these developments?

Organic and fairly traded food are currently a luxury. Because they are relatively expensive compared to food produced by modern conventional methods, people tend to buy them only when they have extra money. When the credit crunch first made itself felt in 2008, spending on organic food was one of the first things to feel the pinch. However, it appears that we are actually living greener lives as a result of this financial hardship. We may no longer buy the 'greenest' food, but people are also moving house less, buying fewer white goods, going on fewer foreign holidays and driving less.[23] Our level of disposable income seems to correlate directly with the damage we do to the planet (see Chapter 6).

The global picture is likely to change dramatically in the coming years, as pressure to grow enough food at affordable prices forces producers and consumers to make compromises. Few people care whether their food is organic when even conventionally produced food is expensive – and fewer farmers will grow luxury crops such as coffee when they are starving. These are serious and complex matters that will not be fixed by one or other superficial label. When we pretend they are solvable in this way, we risk making the mistake of the priest in the parable of the good Samaritan, who probably avoided helping the victim because his priestly status meant there were implications in having contact with a dead or dying person (Lev. 21) – also a convenient excuse not to get involved.

Solving global poverty and environmental problems will not be easy. We know that the choices we make in the supermarket and shops have a real effect on others' lives, but it's all too easy to push this fact to the back of our minds by buying one or other quick-fix solution. Not that these are wrong in themselves – Fairtrade, organic, local and other labels all have great potential benefits to producers and the environment. However, we cannot pretend that the problems are simple enough to be reduced to a single dimension. These certifications all reflect good intentions, and do not achieve the same ends. When it appears that there is no 'best' option, the solution is not simply to pick another product with one or other brand or certification, but to find other ways of addressing the problem it represents – through involvement with charities or other initiatives, and by adjusting our lifestyles in different ways. It is only by engaging with the problems, even imperfectly, that we can address them. We need to deepen our engagement and make informed, deliberate decisions about what we are trying to achieve, whether that's workers' rights, social projects, trade justice, or any number of aspects of care for the environment.

Meditation

He upholds the cause of the oppressed and gives food to the hungry. The Lord sets prisoners free, the Lord gives sight to the blind, the Lord lifts up those who are bowed down, the Lord loves the righteous. The Lord watches over the alien and sustains the fatherless and the widow, but he frustrates the ways of the wicked. (Ps. 146.7–9)

Discussion questions

- Which 'ethical' products do you buy, and why?
- What else could you do, or in what other ways could you adjust your lifestyle, to achieve the same ends?
- In which areas of shopping would you like to be able to make better-informed decisions? Choose one to make a priority.

6

Social footprint: our environmental impact

CRITICS BLAST AL GORE'S DOCUMENTARY AS 'REALISTIC'
NEW YORK – The Al Gore-produced global-warming documentary An Inconvenient Truth *is being panned by critics nationwide who claim the 90-plus minute environmental film is 'too disturbingly realistic and well-researched to enjoy.' 'I found it difficult to suspend my disbelief in man-made climate change for the first half-hour – and utterly impossible after that – which makes for a movie-going experience that's far more educational than it is enjoyable,' said New York Post film critic Skip Hack. 'Gore's film overwhelms viewers with staggering amounts of scientific information until nothing about global warming is left to the imagination, and that's just not good entertainment. Two stars.' Some critics have called the film's claims that sea levels could rise 20 feet somewhat sensationalistic, although most agree that this is not enough to save the film from being unwatchably factual.*
From The Onion, *satirical news organization, 31 May 2006*[1]

The earth has limited natural resources, whether we mean non-renewable ones such as fossil fuels, or renewable ones such as water, rainforest, or fish stocks. Renewable resources can't be consumed beyond their rate of regeneration for very long without seriously affecting their future production and even existence; non-renewable resources such as coal, oil and natural gas only regenerate on an almost inconceivably long-term geological timescale, if at all, and their consumption must be considered alongside the need to come up with viable alternatives by the time they are depleted.

The degree to which burning fossil fuels affects climate change is still a topic of hot debate among scientists, politicians and the public. Many eminent scientists have concluded that significant global warming is unavoidable as a result of carbon dioxide emissions, and that this will have profound effects, including altered climate patterns and weather events, rising sea levels, effects on food production and water supply, and effects on health[2] – though others are more sceptical about the degree of change we can expect, and occasionally even about whether climate change can be attributed to human factors at all.[3] Although there is as yet no definitive consensus on the level of human-caused climate change we will experience, it is clear from a whole range of issues, from deforestation to overfishing, that our current failure to use finite resources sustainably demands immediate action.

The Jubilee laws of Leviticus, chapter 25, ensured that every Israelite down the generations would retain access to their family's share of land, and therefore to food and income. These laws, seemingly so far removed from the model of our present economy, have modern-day relevance in the context of sustainable living and our use of finite natural resources and the effect this has on less privileged people in low-income countries, now and in the future.

Environmental label, personal cost

It's easy to think that environmental issues are beyond our control since, by their nature, they are huge-scale events: 'acts of God' such as tsunamis, earthquakes and hurricanes that can't be addressed by individuals. This is also true of pollution and the depletion of natural resources which, because they take place on a national or even global level, seem beyond the power of any one person or group of people to deal with. Even whole countries will not make a difference if the others don't get in line as well. Our efforts – or our individual habits – are a drop in the ocean, and pale into insignificance when viewed in the context of the world's almost seven billion inhabitants, or even the UK's 60-odd million. It's tempting to believe that only if wide-scale change occurs, through government intervention and international legislation, will any measures prove effective.

> 'The Senate is now considering increasing government subsidies for corn growers to produce more ethanol. If we produce enough ethanol we can postpone our next invasion of a Middle Eastern country for two to three years.'   Jay Leno, talk-show host

However much the facts of unsustainable living are stated in economic or scientific terms (degrees centigrade per century, dollars per barrel, acres of rainforest per year, millimetres of sea-level, parts per million of pollutants), how we treat our planet is really a question of justice. Environmental issues are closely linked to social ones: however distant the effects of our consumer lifestyles seem to us, they do have real, measurable consequences. It is a poignant reality that although the cause is overwhelmingly the responsibility of the already wealthy and privileged, globally speaking, the effects tend to cost most to those who have little to start with – for example, through deforestation, intensive farming and high water-use to farm cash crops for export in low-income countries, and the knock-on environmental damage this causes. In addition, the faster we use fossil fuels without developing alternatives, the fewer resources we will leave for future generations at home or abroad.

Levels of carbon emissions highlight the inequalities in the distribution of resources. 'More than half the global emissions of greenhouse gases are produced by less than one-sixth of the world population'; in terms of climate change, the effects fall hardest on the most vulnerable:

> A consequence of [global warming] is the likely increase in extreme weather events – hurricanes, floods at one extreme, droughts and heat waves at the other. The physical effects fall disproportionately on the very young and very old, on the poor and the marginalised in places such as sub-Saharan Africa. One quarter of the world's population live in poverty, with a marginal lifestyle that is vulnerable to changes caused by drought or flooding, by the failure of agricultural crops, or by rising sea levels.[4]

Personal choices

As argued in Chapter 7, we bear responsibility for the investments we allow to be made with our money. If we bank or invest our money unethically, or even unthinkingly, that has real consequences. The money might be used to buy real guns and ammunition, fund real deaths, cut down real rainforest or displace real people. That we don't ask, don't directly know those involved, or that this would still happen (even to a slightly lesser degree) without our investment, doesn't negate the fact that we are still accountable for what is funded. The same is true of unsustainable living: our habits of consumption have real consequences for others. There is a link between cause and effect that makes it impossible to deny responsibility. That we have plenty of partners in crime is hardly an excuse.

Viewed as a series of vast global phenomena, it is no wonder that people claim to feel helpless about making any real impact on environmental issues. In fact it's often tempting to frame the problems in these terms to draw attention away from the intricate mosaic of apparently trivial, everyday choices that each of us makes, and that each impact our energy use. The problem:

> is not one vast, impersonal challenge, but rather billions of tiny, personal ones. It is your full boiling kettle in the morning, your daily drive to work, your weekly supermarket shop, your bi-annual holiday. It is a thousand things we do without thinking: everyday behaviour that we assume, quite wrongly, is a normal part of life and therefore sustainable.[5]

The impact of carbon emissions on climate change has not been precisely quantified, although it would be surprising if the extreme sceptics were proved right in thinking it has no effect at all. However, levels of carbon emissions also reflect fossil-fuel consumption: the rate at which finite resources are being burned for good. At present global rates of consumption (which are likely to rise in the near future), and with the reserves currently proved to exist, there are perhaps 60 years of natural gas and 130 years of coal left. Oil reserves might last only another 40 years.[6] This is soon enough to be of immediate concern for most people now, let alone the next generation. There is also the fact that prices of all fossil fuels will rise sharply as supplies dwindle and extraction costs rise.

> 'Why should I care about future generations? What have they ever done for me?'
> Groucho Marx

As an indication of the way current fossil-fuel use is distributed, average CO_2 emissions per person in the USA are around 20 tonnes per year. The UK figure is nine tonnes. India's figure is one tonne, and those of very low-income countries may be as low as a tenth of a tonne. Northern America, which has a population of 330 million (5 per cent of the world's population), is responsible for almost 20 per cent of global greenhouse gas emissions; the EU, with a population of around 500 million (7 per cent), is responsible for nearly 15 per cent. With 0.9 per cent of the world's population, the UK is responsible for 2 per cent of current greenhouse gas emissions. There are huge inequalities in the way the world's remaining resources are being used, and in the resulting pollution they cause.

In the UK, as in most industrialized countries, energy consumption is split roughly evenly across three categories: domestic, transport and industry/service.[7] Of course, we are all responsible for a share of all of these since we all live somewhere, travel and purchase goods and services to some extent. But it's our immediate personal choices that tend to be the most fuel-costly and damaging – therefore also the areas in which the biggest changes can be made.

Domestic

The figures for domestic energy consumption are surprising. On average, over half (56 per cent) is used for heating (or cooling) space, and almost a quarter (23 per cent) for heating water – accounting for nearly 80 per cent of the total. Appliances use another 13 per cent, cooking 5 per cent and lighting 3 per cent.[8] Space heating illustrates recent changes in attitudes; in 1970, when 31 per cent of houses had central heating, the average home temperature was 12.6° C. In 2001, when 90 per cent had central heating, the average temperature was 18.9° C.[9]

Transport

The way and amount we travel makes the same point. Some 42 per cent of CO_2 emissions from transport come from passenger cars, while aviation accounts for 21 per cent. Public transport accounts for just 4 per cent. The remaining third of emissions are from HGVs (17 per cent), light-duty vehicles (10 per cent) and shipping (6 per cent). Air travel is expected to rise sharply in the coming years: a series of airport expansions are planned, despite government climate-change targets. Some analysts predict that without major technological changes or changes to our flying habits, air travel alone could swallow up the UK's entire carbon budget by 2050.[10]

I'd use public transport if it wasn't so expensive. But driving across the country costs less than taking the train – even for one person. Taking the plane can sometimes be even cheaper than that. It seems crazy, but there's just no financial incentive to be green at the moment.

Jan, 32

Despite the fact that fuel efficiency has increased, from around 29 mpg (9.7 l/100 km) for new cars in 1978 to 37 mpg (7.63 l/100 km) in 2002,[11] overall transport energy consumption nearly doubled from 1970 to 2001, largely due to increases in road and air traffic. Private cars and taxis account for 80 per cent of the UK's yearly 310 billion mile (500 billion km) motor-vehicle miles travelled.[12]

Industry

Our purchasing habits complete the picture of resource overuse. Gross Domestic Product (GDP) has doubled since the 1970s. Disposable income has risen, but despite this, people are saving less and borrowing has increased sharply, now standing at £1.46 trillion, of which £231 billion is unsecured debt – an average of £21,500 per household.[13] All of this means that we are spending more and saving less than we used to. The manufacturing, packaging and transport of all this buying takes its toll on the environment.

What we eat comprises a surprisingly high proportion of CO_2 emissions. Food, drink and tobacco account for over seven tonnes per year, or nearly a third of household emissions.[14] Some 3.5 per cent of total CO_2 emissions are caused by transporting the food to the shops and supermarkets within the UK (and our driving to buy it causes another 1 per cent). If it has come from abroad, even this amount is only a fraction of total production factors (aside from transporting the food from supplier to consumer, these include the carbon costs of running agricultural machinery, producing fertilizer and feeds, and perhaps heating greenhouses).

Consumer culture and the environment

A vast proportion of fossil-fuel use, pollution and greenhouse-gas emissions come from choices we make almost without thinking. Many are based on convenience or habit or lifestyle factors that are otherwise undesirable as they are ultimately damaging to our well-being. One common and apparently trivial example is the 'standby' function on many electrical goods, such as TVs, stereos and VCR/DVD players. It has been estimated that electrical appliances left on standby account for 7 billion kWh of electricity, representing more than 4 million tonnes of CO_2 annually[15] – around 1 per cent of total UK emissions.[16] The purpose of these is primarily so that we can avoid the nuisance of an unnecessary trip to the socket or appliance. Mobile phone chargers, laptop adaptors and other transformers are also often left plugged in unnecessarily, and therefore using power, when not in use.

Unfortunately, the issue goes far deeper than a little couch-potato laziness. The ways that our society has changed for the better since the Second World War have also brought problems. As affluence has grown, so has consumption: we spend not only because we need to, but because we want to. Alongside that, mobility and family break-down have taken their toll. Our lives are more fragmented, rootless and referenceless. Damage to our networks of relationships and increased wealth have resulted in increased individualism, with its associated environmental costs. We travel further, and rely more on ourselves and less on friends, family and community. We are more likely to live alone. Around 13 per cent of the population lived on their own in England in 2006, four times more than in 1960. Currently around a third of all households are single-occupancy. This is predicted to rise to nearly 40 per cent over the next 20 years. The fastest-increasing category is 25–44-year-olds, and particularly never-married 35–44-year-old men. Because heating and other categories of energy use do not rise proportionally with further occupants, living alone is generally vastly more carbon (and cash) expensive than living with others: 'one-person householders are the biggest consumers of energy, land and household goods. They consume 38 per cent more products, 42 per cent more packaging, 55 per cent more electricity and 61 per cent more gas per person than an individual in a four-person household.'[17]

> 'There's so much pollution in the air now that if it weren't for our lungs there'd be no place to put it all.'
> *Robert Orben, magician and comedy writer*

The same is true of car use; travelling with another person rather than in a separate car halves personal transport emissions. However:

Attempts to create multiple-occupancy car lanes come up against the stubborn unwillingness of people to share their cars, their personal space: in the US in 2000, only 9 per cent of work trips were made in multi-occupant vehicles, compared with 16 per cent in the 1980s.[18]

Despite the best of reasons for doing otherwise, we are growing increasingly resistant to diluting our autonomy, whether in our homes or cars. At the same time, journeys are getting longer: the average commuter spends 139 hours per year travelling to and from work. Outside London, three quarters of these trips are made by car.[19] Neither is it just long trips to work: nearly a quarter of all car journeys are under two miles.[20]

The convenience culture extends to food as well. Power used for cooking is the only domestic energy-use category to have dropped in the last 30 years, due to demands on our time and the rise of ready meals. However, this is offset by the effects of eating out and the preparation, packaging and transport of these products. Moreover, we expect certain standards in our diet. We eat an unsustainable amount of meat: 50 per cent more than we did 40 years ago, and 50 per cent above the World Health Organization's recommended quantity (which, incidentally, focuses on personal health rather than the health of the planet). Global meat production is expected almost to double by 2050 over 2001 levels, as low-income countries catch up to Western levels of consumption.[21] We demand perfect and exotic fruit and veg all year round, despite the fact that these may not be in season or even grown in the UK, and therefore have to be flown or shipped in from abroad or grown in heated greenhouses and kept in refrigerated storage. We reduce the moral value of purchasing goods and services to the question of whether or not we can afford it financially. There is a higher price to pay, but a consumerist mentality ignores this because it doesn't appear on the label and interferes with our right to buy whatever we can afford.

Environmental cost, relational symptom

The increases in mobility, individualism and consumerism the West has seen over the last 50 years have fuelled unsustainable lifestyles. These material benefits have not led to greater happiness – arguably the opposite. The ability and therefore expectation to travel has separated people from their families and communities as they move for work, university and other reasons. We travel further and we tend to travel alone in our cars. Instead of walking to the local shops, we drive to the out-of-town supermarket. Over half of us don't know our neighbours' names;[22] with long working hours and isolating commutes, we don't get the opportunity to meet, and even if we do there often doesn't seem much point in getting to know people because there's little time to meet up and one or other of us might well be moving on soon anyway.

> 'Going out isn't much fun. I've been here a year and I still don't know that many people here.'
> 'Why don't you come out and meet some then?!'
> 'Well, it seems like a lot of hassle. I know I'm probably moving again for work in six months, so there doesn't seem like much point going to the trouble.' Richard, 28

Living alone is far more relationally and environmentally unsound than sharing a house with others, and not just in terms of heating and lighting. Think of all the embodied energy (the energy used to manufacture a product) and power consumption of TVs and stereos, not to mention the materials that go into building houses in the first place. It's a curious thought that every evening up and down your street, there are likely to be dozens of people sitting at home on their own, many of them lonely, each in their own house, on their own sofa, in front of their own TVs, *watching exactly the same programmes* – all in complete isolation from each other. There is a relational and environmental solution there, waiting for people to put it into practice. Christians have a duty to each other and to creation to take the initiative. If house-sharing seems a step too far to begin with, inviting someone over to watch a favourite TV programme is hardly a challenging start.

Unsustainable living is closely, if not inherently, linked to the changing patterns and attitudes about our relationships. That's not to say that environmental problems will fix themselves on their own if only we could sort out our relationships. However, treated in isolation without a radically different approach to the factors that fuel them, there is little chance of lasting impact on the environmental concerns of our age.

Sustainable living: a biblical approach

Understanding sustainable living as primarily an issue of justice, rather than one of technology, politics or economics, shifts responsibility back towards us rather than solely on to governments, businesses and scientists.

Zechariah 7.9–10 reads, 'This is what the LORD Almighty says: "Administer true justice; show mercy and compassion to one another. Do not oppress the fatherless, the alien or the poor. In your hearts do not think evil of each other."' The Bible shows the most concern for those who are already marginalized and at risk of oppression, mentioning the poor over 300 times. The Hebrew word for poor, $^{a}n\bar{a}v\hat{\imath}m$, does not simply mean materially poor, but carries a sense of humility, affliction and weakness, frequently used in contrast to the arrogance of the rich who exploit them. It is an uncomfortable truth that we fall squarely in the latter category.

> Africans live by the mercy of God, otherwise what we call our take home pay cannot really take us home. In a country like Nigeria where the minimum wage is 7,500 Naira [c. $55 per month] and with an average family of six, I wonder how I will take care of them. Little wonder people choose to live by this formula: breakfast, no lunch and a little for dinner with no consideration for the nutritional content of the food. Getting two jobs is almost impossible in Africa. Until there is a change in the economy, system of government and the mentality of the people, poverty will remain a persistent thing.
>
> Alexander, Nigeria[23]

Beyond this social agenda, the environment is worth caring for in its own right, apart from any human impact. Genesis states that the world God created was 'very good' (1.31), and he charged humans with stewarding it (2.15). The fact that the world belongs to God is underlined elsewhere: 'The earth is the LORD's, and everything in it' (Ps. 24.1); 'Through him all things were made; without him nothing was made that has been made' (John 1.3). Against the argument that God created the world only for our benefit, solely as a vehicle for our interactions with him and with other people, Job 38–39 shows that he cares for the earth independently of humanity. God makes the point that the earth was here before humans were made, and they had no part to play in its creation and cannot control its environmental processes.

The Jubilee laws provide a useful perspective on the world's wider resources. Leviticus chapter 25 describes a sustainable society in which everyone had access to a share of what we now call 'natural capital'. In the Old Testament, this meant productive land for growing crops and keeping livestock. Nowadays we might understand this more broadly – not only in terms of an equal share of the world's productive land for food, but also in terms of a sustainable energy budget. The rate at which we consume remaining reserves of fossil fuels must be balanced against a long-term strategy that takes into account pollution, climate change and the development of suitable alternative energy supplies.

Why act?

For Christians, the first reason why we should care about the environment is that God cares for the environment. Gratitude is the only appropriate response to God's gift of creation: carrying out the task of stewarding the earth that he gave us at the beginning. Beyond this, there are many other pragmatic reasons to live within our environmental means. Wasting natural resources now simply means there will be less to use in future, whether this affects us or future generations. Overreliance on fossil fuels places us in a vulnerable position when we cannot obtain them, either because supplies run out or because producing countries limit them artificially, as has been the case as a result of disputes between Russia and the Ukraine.

> 'My grandfather rode a camel, my father rode a camel, I drive a Mercedes, my son drives a Land Rover, his son will drive a Land Rover, but his son will ride a camel.'
>   Sheikh Rashid bin Saeed Al Maktoum, former Emir of Dubai

If projections for the impact of climate change prove correct, there will be further problems. Although the first effects will be felt by those in low-income countries – particularly the large number of people who live close to sea level or near rivers and are therefore acutely at risk from flooding – environmental disaster is something that will affect all of us, both directly and indirectly, as unpredictable and severe weather events increase, impacting power supplies, homes and food production both in the UK and abroad. The Stern Review on the Economics of Climate Change, released at the end of 2006, examined the possible impact on the world economy of climate change. The Review:

> estimates that if we don't act, the overall costs and risks of climate change will be equivalent to losing at least 5 per cent of global GDP each year, now and forever. If a wider range of risks and impacts is taken into account, the estimates of damage could rise to 20 per cent of GDP or more. In contrast, the costs of action – reducing greenhouse gas emissions to avoid the worst impacts of climate change – can be limited to around 1 per cent of global GDP each year.[24]

Although the report drew mixed reactions and it ultimately remains uncertain to what extent human activity might prevent the climate from changing, this estimate has since been revised upwards to 2 per cent of GDP, to reflect raised expectations that we will see more severe weather events in the years ahead.

Even without this factor, there are good reasons to act now. Primarily, this is an opportunity to examine our lives, pinpointing those areas in which addressing environmental problems will also have relational benefits, as well as the obvious financial ones (saving power means saving money too). One thing the credit crunch and global recession have prompted is a reassessment of debt-driven consumerism – a realization that the acquisition of more and more stuff based on cheap credit cannot go on indefinitely, and that there is more to life than buying things. Needless to say, this does not require an economic crisis to remain true. Life does not consist in the abundance of possessions (Luke 12.15).

On purely pragmatic grounds, the world as a whole is consuming resources 30 per cent faster than they are being regenerated, the USA consuming six times its sustainable share. Because of the increase expected from emerging economies, it is expected that 'by 2030, if nothing changes, mankind would need two planets to sustain its lifestyle.'[25] Sooner or later, it is inevitable that we will have to start living within our means: there is no other choice. Even lawmakers are moving in that direction, albeit slowly and reluctantly. Particularly given the other benefits, it's best to adapt to that situation while we can, before we simply have to.

Non-fixes

The dangers posed by humanity's impact on the environment, among which many, such as soil erosion and extinction of species, are regularly overshadowed by the carbon debate, demand far-reaching changes to our attitudes and behaviour that will not occur overnight. In the meantime, 'solutions' such as carbon trading are being discussed that raise more questions than they answer.

Carbon trading is the practice by which companies or countries that pollute above their allowance are able to purchase spare 'credits' from those who have not used their allowance. Although this may provide a partial and short-term solution, it can never be a complete answer. It may 'lower' individual countries' carbon foot-print, but the world as a whole already exceeds its carbon budget, and fossil fuel usage is set to increase as low-income countries industrialize.

In addition, carbon trading and similar schemes essentially suggest that it is legitimate to pay for bad behaviour by purchasing some latitude from those worse off. It's a way of buying ourselves out of injustice; something that we would hardly consider moral in other circumstances – for example, paying someone else to take points on a driving licence, or the medieval Church's practice of selling 'indulgences' to pardon sins. What begins as a penalty can quickly develop into an accepted price tag, removing the moral stigma of pollution and reducing it to an economic issue. The trade-off between the environment and the economy is a false one, if the Stern report is even half right.

Similarly, 'techno-fixes' – the idea that improvements in technology and efficiency will provide answers to our demands for resources – are unlikely to be the ultimate solution. Such improvements cannot be assumed, especially in the short timescale required for effective action. New techniques and processes (such as clean and renewable power, or carbon-capture technology) may help, *if* they accompany a change in attitudes and behaviour. If they don't, there's a good chance they will actually make the problem worse: evidence suggests that the 'rebound effect' can offset any potential gains. Cheaper power means people feel that they can use more electricity; more fuel-efficient engines mean that they feel justified in driving further and that manufacturers build more powerful cars; better-insulated houses remove some of the guilt in turning the central heating up higher.

> *'Don't get me wrong: I love nuclear energy! It's just that I prefer fusion to fission. And it just so happens that there's an enormous fusion reactor safely banked a few million miles from us. It delivers more than we could ever use in just about eight minutes. And it's wireless!'*   William McDonough, architect and designer

Viewed in these terms, unsustainable living is a temporary technical problem that will inevitably be overcome by scientific advances. While it's possible that technology may one day provide unlimited cheap and clean power (perhaps via nuclear fusion), the issue is not primarily a technological but rather a moral one. It's not a barrier to be overcome but an indication that we are living the wrong way. Relational issues are not amenable to techno-fixes, whatever the mobile phone companies claim. Expecting technology to fix the symptom without addressing the root cause is like accepting a liver transplant without giving up the drinking that caused the problem in the first place.

Global problems, personal solutions

Understanding sustainable living as a matter of justice suddenly changes the issue from a vast, diffuse and ungraspable one to a personal and relational one. This is important because it shifts the burden squarely on to us and our everyday decisions: the journeys we undertake, the conveniences and appliances we use, the things we buy, the assumptions we make and the ways we conform to society's expectations.

We need a more holistic approach to sustainable living – one that takes into account our habitual, everyday decisions rather than token gestures. Installing energy-saving light bulbs is a small step in the right direction, but the 1 per cent of total energy use this saves is meaningless if we decide on an extra flight abroad that year. The fact that the government claims to pursue a green agenda but then approves airport expansion and ignores the environmental (let alone social) effects of relationship breakdown is another example of this double-think.

The relational implications of environmental choices mean that sustainable living can be a positive experience rather than a process of denial. One example of both cutting emissions and strengthening relationships would be to re-restrict Sunday trading hours, allowing couples, families and friends more time together while decreasing the shops' carbon footprint. Living with other people rather than alone also has great environmental and relational benefits.

Whatever the personal benefits, sustainable living is at heart an issue of justice. 'Those of us who live in the high-income industrialized nations with standards of living purchased through profligate use of natural resources have a particular responsibility in our stewardship.'[26]

Meditation

From everyone who has been given much, much will be demanded; and from the one who has been entrusted with much, much more will be asked.   (Luke 12.48)

Discussion questions

- Why should the environment be a concern for Christians?
- What are the areas of your life that you think cause most harm to the environment, and why?
- What could you do to change these? Specifically, are there solutions that are both environmental and relational?

7

Worship with wealth

———— ◆•◆•◆ ————

In the early 1980s, the USA experienced a severe recession. High oil prices caused by unrest in the Middle East in the 1970s pushed inflation up to 13.5 per cent by 1980, prompting the Federal Reserve to raise interest rates sharply to bring it back under control, but reducing economic growth in the process. At the same time, public unease was further agitated by Soviet propaganda following Russia's successful development of the neutron bomb, which uses high levels of radiation to kill people without damaging buildings or equipment. Talk-show host Johnny Carson combined these two popular news stories when he joked on The Tonight Show *that 'Scientists have developed a powerful new weapon that destroys people but leaves buildings standing. It's called the 17 per cent interest rate.' From today's perspective, high interest rates proved to have the far greater impact.*

This chapter explores some of our common assumptions about money, and tries to look at money from a biblical perspective. As a result, it's probably the most challenging chapter in the book. Needless to say, any thoughts here don't constitute formal financial advice, and all the usual disclaimers apply.

> 'For where your treasure is, there your heart will be also.'
> *Matthew 6.21*

Martin Luther spoke of three levels of conversion: the conversion of the mind, the conversion of the heart and finally the hardest, the conversion of the wallet. Engaging with money can often be a difficult area for Christians. Sometimes it can appear remote to our faith, even irrelevant. Or maybe an interest in investment and making money seems distasteful. After all, the poor are blessed while the rich have already received their comfort (Luke 6.20, 24). The Gospels are full of examples of rich men whose wealth was a barrier to the kingdom of God. In the Old Testament, the rich are frequently denounced by the prophets as oppressors of the poor, at whose expense they have made their fortunes. Few people actively and intentionally want to be poor, but perhaps not paying too much attention to our savings and investments is the next best thing.

> '*The median income in the UK is around £377 per week. The half of us who earn less than this might feel badly off, until you realize that this figure puts you in the top 4.3 per cent of the richest people in the world. If you earn the average (mean) of £24,000 per year, you're in the top 2 per cent, and if you're a higher-rate taxpayer you're in the top 1 per cent. Someone on UK minimum wage falls in the top 11 per cent. Even someone on benefits falls in the top 15 per cent.*'[1]

Wealth comes with clear spiritual warnings attached. Some readers might think this area doesn't apply to them as they have no spare cash to 'invest', but the reality that the USA and UK are two of the wealthiest countries in the world should make that an impossible point of view to argue without deluding ourselves. Everyone will almost certainly have to steward some combination of bank balances, overdrafts, mortgages, pensions, savings, shares, credit card debt and unsecured loans over the course of his or her life.

Wealth isn't inherently bad. Jesus was supported by a number of independently wealthy women, and Nicodemus and Joseph of Arimathea weren't told to give up their money when they came to faith. On the other hand, the rich ruler of Luke 18.18–30 allowed his wealth to compete with the kingdom of God for his loyalty, so it had to go. The answer to the tensions of faith and wealth is *not* to keep our money at arm's length, pushing it to the back of our minds to ensure that storing up treasures for ourselves on earth (Matt. 6.19) doesn't gain unwarranted influence over our thoughts and motivations.

When we pay either too much or too little attention to our finances, we're missing the Bible's message on the subject. *Nothing* is supposed to be disconnected from our faith, including money; it doesn't exist in a separate sphere that has no bearing on the rest of our Christian life, or on other people. Money itself has no intrinsic moral value, but what we do with it certainly does. It can either further justice or work against it; rarely, if ever, can its use be entirely neutral. If we have money in a bank account, that bank is doing something with it to earn us interest. What does it say about us that the majority of people have little idea what that is?

> *'If you want to know what God thinks about money, just look at the people he gives it to.'* Dorothy Parker

The biblical economy

Some of the things we take for granted look very different when viewed through the lens of the Bible's teaching. Israel's agriculture-based economy was completely unlike ours, but we can learn a lot from the economic values described in the Old Testament. Although this chapter is concerned mainly with how we use our money as individual Christians rather than with restructuring the entire economy around biblical principles, how the Israelite economy functioned is helpful when it comes to understanding what was considered important and what was not.[2] While economic reform on a large scale might be desirable, it is unlikely to be achievable in the short term – meaning that if Christians want to approach these matters in a biblical way, they have to do so for the moment within the existing system.

Perhaps the most surprising fact about Israel's economy was that charging interest was completely prohibited between Israelites. This is stated three times in the Torah alone (Exod. 22.25, Lev. 25.35–37, Deut. 23.19–20). When lending to each other, they were not supposed to benefit materially from the transaction. Interest is the lubricating oil of our debt-based economy, but the prophets considered charging interest to be as sinful as robbery, adultery and idolatry (Ezek. 18.7–8).

> *'Make money your god and it will plague you like the devil.'* Henry Fielding

The Bible is full of verses that explain why interest was so hated. Ezekiel lists it with other acts of oppression and injustice (22.12).

Proverbs 28.8 reads, 'He who increases his wealth by "bite" and "increase" amasses it for another, who will be kind to the poor.'[3] ('Bite' – Hebrew *neshek* – and 'increase' – Hebrew *tarbîth* – are two different words for interest commonly used in the Bible. The Talmud suggests that the lender 'bites' the borrower in the course of receiving his own 'increase' – that is, they refer to the same transaction from different points of view.) The suggestion is that interest was a means by which the rich extracted money from the poor. Interest is often mentioned in the context of poverty. Nehemiah criticized his countrymen who were charging interest at the expense of their already poverty-stricken neighbours, calling for lending to continue but interest payments to be returned. (The rate of 1 per cent in Nehemiah 5.11 was probably monthly, not yearly.)

> I was on a low income. I borrowed a few hundred pounds for clothes for the children, food and utility bills. I met the man through friends, who said they knew someone who'd lend me money. They didn't tell you how much interest you'd pay. You think they're a friend, you don't know any different. Soon I was paying £1,000 a month. I didn't have any money left for myself. Then I borrowed more money off them again. I was paying them with my benefits and disability money. I had to make sure I paid them all the time. If I had enough money to buy food I would, if not, I'd go without. It was never ending, the loans were never coming down. Victim of loan shark[4]

Lending freely to the poor is closely linked with teaching to cancel debts regularly. The effect of many loans today is to push people who are struggling financially even further into long-term debt and poverty through compounding interest payments – an exploitative result of something that, biblically, only existed to relieve poverty. In the Bible, poverty was supposed to be temporary, not an opportunity for richer people to make an income. Deuteronomy 15.4–5 promises that there will be 'no poor among you'. It is no coincidence that these verses follow the law about cancelling debt every seven years.

However, while poverty – particularly crippling, long-term poverty – was an awful situation to be in, the Bible also stresses the importance of paying debts. Debtors would offer security for the loan they received, or even sell themselves into servitude in the event of default. (This, too, was limited to seven years, meaning that permanent bond-service, like permanent debt and poverty, should not become a feature of Israel.) Therefore interest as a form of compensation was not paid.

> 'Those who understand compound interest are destined to collect it. Those who don't are doomed to pay it.'   Anon.

The Old Testament ban on interest applies to *all* interest, not just 'excessive interest' or 'usury' as some versions translate it. Loans were supposed to be for those in dire need. To charge interest would be to increase their financial burden, particularly if future earnings do not cover the repayments, allowing compound interest to take its course. It reinforces inequality of wealth distribution, making the rich even richer at the price of keeping others permanently in debt.[5]

Commercial interest

The same principle is harder to understand of a commercial loan – such as a loan we might take out from a bank today to start a new business. If a loan is productive to a business, some interest as a share of profits seems reasonable. However, loans between Israelites that could have been productive (such as farmers loaning seed) must have existed, but were also included in the ban. Although Exodus 22.25 and Leviticus 25.35–37 mention interest in the context of a loan to the poor, Deuteronomy 23.19–20 states that *every* 'brother Israelite' is covered. The only exception is for foreigners (Deut. 23.20), who could be charged interest. Some commentators see this as a form of continuing 'Holy War' against the surrounding nations. However, a more likely reason is that if there were no reciprocal arrangements, Israelites would be open to exploitation from foreigners who did not share their economic law.[6] They would be charged interest by others, or their interest-free loan could be used to gain a profit at interest (an Old Testament version of the modern-day practice of 'stoozing', in which money borrowed on a credit card at a zero per cent introductory rate is invested for profit).

The question is, *why* is interest – especially interest on commercial loans – considered inherently morally wrong? Part of the reason may be that money is 'fungible': it's easy to move around and exchange for other commodities. It's very difficult to know what a loan might be used for; money could be exchanged for wheat, but who knows whether that would be for consumption or planting? Particularly in Israel's agriculture-based economy, there would be less distinction between personal and commercial loans. Needless to say, the highly leveraged companies common today – those that borrow heavily to increase their returns – weren't a feature of the biblical economy.

The Old Testament ban on interest is strongly worded and comprehensive. Contrary to a superficial reading, Jesus doesn't overturn this law in the parable of the ten minas (Luke 19.11–27),[7] in which a series of servants are judged on the return they gain from an investment. The first ones are praised when they 'put this money to work' as commanded, while the last hides his master's money and is duly punished.

> Then another servant came and said, 'Sir, here is your mina; I have kept it laid away in a piece of cloth. I was afraid of you, because you are a hard man. You take out what you did not put in and reap what you did not sow.' His master replied, 'I will judge you by your own words, you wicked servant! You knew, did you, that I am a hard man, taking out what I did not put in, and reaping what I did not sow? Why then didn't you put my money on deposit, so that when I came back, I could have collected it with interest?'

Jesus confirms the Old Testament teaching. Collecting interest is exactly what a 'hard man' would be expected to do: taking out what he did not put in and reaping what he did not sow. If that's true, it's a huge challenge to Christians. Most of us look around for the best rates on bank accounts and credit cards without thinking twice.

This idea of reaping where we haven't sown sheds light on why even commercial interest payments were considered unjust. These loans require repayment at the agreed interest rate, regardless of the profitability of the business. If the business does well, the creditor receives the flat rate, notwithstanding his money has enabled another to gain greater wealth. On the other hand, if the business makes a loss, the same interest payments on the loan are still required, making the business more likely to fail. In the event of collapse, the money must still be repaid.[8] The creditor gains from the venture without assuming any of the risk. And by expecting a fixed return, both creditor and debtor make a presumption of future success – the folly of which the Bible points out more than once (e.g. James 4.13–16, Prov. 27.1).

> The credit crunch has ruined my business. Things were going really well until I lost one of my biggest clients. I asked banks for a loan to tide me over while I looked for new clients and ways to cut back on costs, but their rates were prohibitively expensive – if they were willing to lend at all. I had to terminate the lease on my office and make my staff redundant, which meant I had to pay them too. I can't even get started again because I can't access credit to purchase supplies.
>
> David, 43

Commercial loans aren't biblically wrong because they're necessarily exploitative (as exacting interest from the poor would be) but because they make presumptions about the future and fail to incentivize a long-term relationship between providers and users of funds; in fact, they place all risk on the borrower. There's also a disconnection between risk and return: the payments are *unrelated* to the productivity of the loan. On the other hand, equity partnerships, in which the investor owns a stake in the business, share both risk and reward, and there is a close link between investment and return.

In the worst cases, long-term interest payments may be required just to stop a loan growing any further. US national debt is currently over $11 trillion; interest payments on this total over $450 billion per year, or around 19 per cent of all tax receipts. Interest on UK government debt is projected to stand at £42.9 billion for 2010–11, or more than the defence budget.[9] By 2013–14, when government debt will have risen to £1.37 trillion, interest payments alone could be £58 billion,[10] the fourth-largest spending category after social security, health and education. This is one reason to avoid government bonds as a form of investment. They might seem safe, but they effectively defer taxation rises on to future years and generations by bailing out past and present governments' overspending. One day our children will decide that we have lived well at their expense – in effect, mortgaging their future.

Principles of investing

Though our economy is different from the Bible's, some of the principles behind the biblical economy – principles intended to maintain justice and equality – can still be used to assess various different types of investment. In addition, there are a number of other factors we can take into account from further biblical laws surrounding trade and business.

The first thing to remember is that where money changes hands, there is a relationship – even a brief and all-but-anonymous one through intermediaries and computers. That transaction is unlikely to be morally neutral. If someone is making money, that money has to come from somewhere – or, more accurately, someone.

Responsibility

When we invest our money (whether in a bank, shares, pension, directly in a business or in any other way) we are enabling its use for certain ends. These ends may or may not be beneficial to individuals, society as a whole or the environment. In many cases, investors will not even know what is being done with their money, either because they don't know exactly how the business (e.g. a bank) makes its money to pay them interest, or because they do not know where their money is going in the first place. If shares or a pension are dealt with through a pensions company and/or a fund manager, there may be little choice or knowledge of where the money is invested at all.

God has given us stewardship over all of the world's resources but we are accountable for how we use them. While the link between our investments and their knock-on effects can seem remote thanks to layers of mediation, we cannot overlook the harm being done with our money, even if not with our explicit knowledge. This may include arms dealing, tobacco, alcohol or pornography industries, animal testing or harmful environmental policies, child labour or exploitative practices towards workers.

> Every month I invest in a FTSE-100 tracker fund. I was advised that it was a good investment, because these are big, relatively safe companies, and the stock market has always outperformed interest rates over the long term. But when I thought about it harder, I realized there were probably a few in that hundred that I wouldn't like. Along with property, utility and healthcare companies, I'm also investing in British American Tobacco and Imperial Tobacco, Oil and Mining companies with practices I think are harmful to the environment, and others I'd

question whether I'd want to invest in directly for various reasons. But
that was never mentioned in the advice I got.   Hugh, 36

'It is contradictory to bemoan economic exploitation of low-income
countries and yet fail to realize that our interest and pensions are
being secured by the same exploitation perpetrated in the name of
shareholders and bondholders.'[11] Finding out what our bank deposits
and shares are used to fund, and changing our accounts if necessary,
is the least we should be doing.

Debt

Responsibility for what is done 'in our name' with our money extends
to the issue of debt. The Bible takes the obligation to pay our debts
seriously: where a debtor defaulted, he might lose his security or
potentially even be sold into servitude to pay what he owed. The
seriousness of debt is demonstrated by Jesus' use of it as an image
of sin, as in the Lord's Prayer and explicitly in the parable of the
unmerciful servant in Matthew 18.21–35. Unpaid debt is viewed as
a great injustice. Psalm 37.21 reads, 'The wicked borrow and do not
repay, but the righteous give generously.' While this may not immediately appear to pose a problem to the investor (who presumably
has spare money rather than debt, as relative interest rates mean that
it is rarely profitable to borrow in order to invest, or to invest while
debts are still outstanding),[12] it can have other implications. Limited
liability means that shareholders are not obliged to pay their debts
in the case of a company failing: their losses are limited to their
original investment. While this may seem fair or good sense, one effect
can be effectively to defraud others of their money. For example,
in October 2006, European Home Retail, parent to the Christmas-
hamper company Farepak, went into administration. Customers who
had saved all year found that no one was under obligation to fulfil
their orders. In 2008 a number of airlines went bankrupt, including
US Skybus Airlines, leaving passengers stranded at airports and forced
to buy new flights home.

Although shareholders have some of the rights of ownership over
the company, they don't share all of the responsibilities, 'including
payment of debts incurred by their enterprise in case of insolvency, or
a duty to compensate communities for decisions adversely affecting
them'.[13] Once again, there's a disconnection between the investor

and the investment – this time in the responsibility that ownership normally entails. When a company is declared insolvent, there is an order in which it is required to pay its debts: tax liabilities first, banks and other financial institutions next, and lastly smaller creditors, consumers, employees and finally shareholders, if there's anything left.

> We've not had a single penny from the administrators at all, which we find very distressing. At no point have we even been contacted to let us know what's been happening. When you look at Northern Rock, within days of that the Government made an announcement that they would be guaranteeing people's money. A year down the line and we've not had anything like that.
>
> Louise McDaid, Farepak victims committee[14]

Under the present system, company decisions are made for the shareholders' (owners') benefit. Nevertheless, shareholders are not accountable for the consequences of these decisions. In the case of large corporations, there may be many unknown shareholders, who have nothing to do with the running of the business. While this protection from total liability has numerous advantages – indeed, much technological and economic progress would not have happened without the investment that limited liability has brought – it also prevents the full exercise of responsibility when things go wrong.

Without major changes in company structure and legislation it's difficult to see how this problem can be overcome. However, for the Christian, the obligation to pay one's debts should be a factor when considering an investment. It might, for example, serve as an extra incentive not to invest in a high-risk or struggling company on the grounds that we would be seeking potential rewards at the risk of imposing debts that we would not be required to pay in the event of failure. Alternatively, it might mean steering clear of equities altogether, and opting for another form of investment, such as property.

Transparency

Financial returns don't come from nowhere.[15] They essentially involve the redistribution of assets: if one person is buying, another is selling. Ideally, both parties will gain from the exchange of goods or services for money. However, just because someone consents to the transaction doesn't make it just.[16] In other words, 'she should have known better', 'he doesn't have a choice' or 'they can afford it' are not justifications for an unfair sale. For example, one writer tells of an American businessman who took advantage of German post-war inflation. 'The head of Abbey Rents in California began his multimillion dollar collection of Bibles in these years; a desperate German sold him an original Gutenberg Bible for $50, American. It is now worth over a million dollars.'[17] Unfortunately, the writer uses this story as an example of desirable prudence and foresight, rather than one of unjustly exploiting a neighbour's dire financial circumstances!

The Bible doesn't limit how much profit is made in any given transaction, but it does ensure that traders didn't make money dishonestly, which would involve an injustice against another person. Therefore gaining riches by exploiting workers, holding back wages[18] or by other unjust means[19] are forbidden, as are more obviously bribery and extortion.[20] The Law specifically bans the use of misleading weights and measures,[21] and the prophets criticize traders for this and other dishonest practices, such as inflating prices and bulking out measures of grain with inedible weight, 'selling even the sweepings with the wheat'.[22]

These laws express principles we usually take for granted today. The buyer should know exactly what he or she is getting for the agreed price, or workers should know that the time and effort they are expending will be rewarded at the agreed rate. In other words, those involved in a transaction have responsibility to each other. The exchange – of goods for money, or money for work – must be transparent. Anything else is dishonesty, and one or other party suffers for it.

While this is taken for granted in shops, it's not always the case elsewhere in the economy. Speculators who intend to buy shares or commodities such as gold, oil or wheat while they are cheap (often with borrowed money) to sell them when the price rises, essentially hope that they have better information or judgement than the person on the other side of the transaction. Their intention is that they will offload a commodity that will shortly be worth less than the sale price, or buy one that will shortly be worth far more, as in the example of the Gutenberg Bible above. Because commodity prices are unpredictable, particularly in the short term, this is not the same as giving a buyer misleading information in order to make a sale.

However, the fact remains that the seller is hoping to profit at the expense of someone less well informed, reaping where he has not sown. That the buyer is hoping to do the same does not excuse this. (In addition, hoarding and commodity speculation can have disastrous effects: in 2008 these received part of the blame for driving up global food prices.[23])

This does not mean that buying low and selling high are inherently wrong: the nature of the relationship between buyer and seller is more important. On the one hand, the seller might be offloading an overpriced commodity before its value plunges, essentially passing on the loss to the unsuspecting buyer. On the other, the buyer might have good reason to accept the asking price, even if it seems high to the seller. The point is that the first transaction is based on the seller's assumption that he knows, or suspects, something the buyer does not, and that he will therefore profit at the buyer's expense. The second transaction is based on both parties having the same information and intentions, neither trying to deceive the other (and both benefiting as a result).[24] That's the kind of transaction that Christians need to make.

Risk and return

What the parable of the ten minas also suggests is that there should be a link between return and risk. Reaping what you have not sown involves collecting a return without risk, or without your money *earning* its additional payment. (In the case of speculation, there is a risk of your investment losing value. However, this risk isn't linked to the potential good your money will do, and doesn't excuse the injustice of profiting at another's expense.)

'Gain all you can, save all you can, give all you can.'
John Wesley, theologian and founder of
the Methodist movement

Hire contracts in the Old Testament confirm this need to keep a link between return and risk. Exodus 22.14–15 reads:

> If a man borrows an animal from his neighbour and it is injured or dies while the owner is not present, he must make restitution . . . If the animal was hired, the money paid for the hire covers the loss.

The owner is providing a service by allowing his neighbour to use the animal. The neighbour will benefit materially, and therefore it is fair that the owner should expect a return on the loan of the animal in the form of rental income. In addition, there is a risk of injury or death to the animal, and the fee contributes towards the cost associated with this. (Over time, on average, fees would accumulate to more than the total cost of replacing the animal.) If, on the other hand, the neighbour is allowed to borrow the animal at no charge – an act of generosity on the part of the owner – he is liable for the full cost if the animal is harmed. The borrower also has responsibility towards the lender, and the lender is not dissuaded from an act of generosity by the thought that he might lose out.

This isn't reaping what has not been sown. The owner of the animal is taking a small risk to provide a service to his neighbour. As such, he is entitled both to a return on his investment and to compensation for the risk he assumes. Both parties know the situation at the beginning, both are expected to benefit from the transaction, and in the case of a mishap at least some responsibility is assumed by the borrower for the loss borne by the owner. The fee for hiring the animal isn't stated by the Bible, presumably being determined on the value of the animal, the level of risk to the owner and the benefit to the borrower.

This seems to validate particular forms of investment where the risk to the owner and benefit to the recipient are intrinsically linked to the financial return. By extension, any lease/hire arrangement, including for property, would be justified by the Exodus rule. On the other hand, the principle of maintaining a clear link between the investment, its utility to others and the risk to the owner, would appear to invalidate those forms of investment in which no benefit is provided to a third party.

Take two examples: investing in property and stock market speculation. Buy-to-let housing appears to be a biblically sound investment. The owner assumes ultimate responsibility for the building (in the case of flood or storm damage, general maintenance and reasonable wear and tear, for example, as well as ultimate ownership, for which he might have a mortgage), but this 'risk' is offset by regular rent payments, and the benefit provided to tenants is rewarded. On the other hand, a speculator isn't using his money for the benefit of the company (and its employees and customers) whose shares he buys – quite the opposite. The intention is essentially to use it to skim cash off the value of the company, saddling someone else with a loss that corresponds to his profit. In some cases, this practice is particularly marked. Some branches of the financial services industry specialize in making enormous gains from short-term movements in share prices. In 2005 the Deputy Chancellor of Germany, Franz Münterfering, said of some hedge fund managers: 'Some financial investors spare no thought for the people whose jobs they destroy. They remain anonymous, have no face, fall like a plague of locusts over our companies, devour everything, then fly on to the next one.'[25] While this caricatures the industry as a whole, it's an apt description of certain practices and mentalities within it. The biblical principles of responsibility, transparency, an investment earning its return through benefit to others and a link between risk and return, are lacking in these circumstances.

Hoarding

Given the number of restrictions on investment, it could be assumed that the most ethical way to provide for the future would be to do nothing with your money and just accumulate it under the mattress until it's needed. But the Bible doesn't sanction hoarding either. James 5.1–6 criticizes rich men who hoard wealth at others' expense. The rich fool in Luke 12.13–21 was condemned for storing up the whole of his bumper harvest for future years, never assuming that he might not be around to enjoy it.[26] Similarly, Psalm 39.6 highlights the case of men who amass wealth for no better reason than the sake of owning it. Hoarding means hiding assets away that could be better used for the benefit of others. This doesn't necessarily mean it should always be given away – although hoarding is a mindset that doesn't sit well with charity. Money well invested is beneficial to the economy, creating jobs and services and therefore improving lives in our community. 'People curse the man who hoards grain, but blessing crowns him who is willing to sell' (Prov. 11.26).

> Dr Karl Menninger once asked a wealthy patient, 'What on earth are you going to do with all that money?' The patient replied, 'Just worry about it, I suppose!' Dr Menninger went on, 'Well, do you get that much pleasure out of worrying about it?' 'No,' responded the patient, 'but I get such terror when I think of giving some of it to somebody.'[27]

Matthew 6.19–21 reads:

> Do not store up for yourselves treasures on earth, where moth and rust destroy, and where thieves break in and steal. But store up for yourselves treasure in heaven, where moth and rust do not destroy, and where thieves do not break in and steal. For where your treasure is, there your heart will be also.

What we do with our money is a good indication of where our true priorities lie. Hoarding ensures only that our money is there for our own benefit, rather than for others – a self-centred rather than outward-focused perspective (see also Luke 16.9). Second, hoarding isn't all that safe. Whereas moth, rust and theft are rarely cause for concern with regards to a bank vault, the same is not true where tax and inflation are future possibilities.

'The trick is to stop thinking of it as "your" money.'

Tax auditor

Most of this chapter has been about what we do with the portion of our income that we do keep, because there are plenty of books and sermons about tithing and giving but comparatively few about investing as a Christian. This is as good a point as any to reiterate that giving *is* important – not just in the good that it can do, but in the way it reminds us where our loyalties really lie.

Asking how we, amid the comfortable distractions of Western life, can retain a sense of urgency and passion in our faith, one missionary writes:

> The early church is instructive on this issue in a number of ways. Acts 4.32 tells us that 'All the believers were one in heart and mind. No one claimed that any of his possessions was his own, but they *shared* everything they had.' What followed? Verses 33–34 show us: 'With great power the apostles continued to testify to the resurrection of the Lord Jesus, and *much grace was upon them all*. There were no needy persons among them.'
>
> The believers were so liberal with their possessions because they knew that their citizenship was in heaven, that Jesus was coming again in judgement, and that it was more important to store up lasting treasures in heaven than selfishly hoard on earth what would in any case ultimately rot and decay. But can you see the correlation between

giving and grace? Was it because the believers were so liberal with their possessions that God was so liberal with his grace?[28]

Relational options

Before deciding how to spend money, we should consider whether there are better ways of achieving the same ends. Many people save or borrow money for specific purposes – buying a car, preparing for a new baby, replacing white goods and so on. Lots of these could be managed just as well through groups of friends and networks within church congregations. Pools of resources can be created for people to borrow from as necessary (such as gardening tools), or items can be circulated as they no longer become useful to the original owners (such as babies' and children's clothes). Where appropriate, such a system could be extended to car-sharing, whether in a larger group or just with one or two other people who pay for insurance, fuel and depreciation as appropriate (not so different from the animal-hire scenario in Exodus 22.14–15).

In circumstances of financial need, individuals or congregations could be encouraged to extend interest-free loans. Although the best situation would be to do this solely on trust, the realities of life mean that some kind of formal process may be necessary, as well as meeting criteria such as length of time/involvement in congregation, references and so on.

As a practical point, if we have spare money to invest as well as mortgage debt, it may be worth paying off the mortgage before investing elsewhere.[29] Although it is reducing debt rather than making a new investment, the net effect is the same. The 'return' may not be as high, but it's tax-free and also contributes to the biblically desirable aim of being debt-free (Rom. 13.8), as well as investing in a physical asset that can be used for others' benefit – either family or tenants. Since we do not know what the future will bring, there is some wisdom to this, particularly if there's an option to take a 'payment holiday' on the debt further down the line, meaning the extra money paid into the mortgage can be offset against future hardship if necessary. Of course, it's also wise to ensure a certain amount of liquidity for emergencies.[30]

I was made redundant last month and have had difficulty finding work since then. I know something will come up eventually but the situation is putting a strain on my relationship. We keep arguing about how we spend what we do have and I'm worried that by the time I do get another job it will be too late for us.   Email to debt counsellor

Financial caretaking and caring for our relationships are more closely linked than we might realize. Money worries are the single biggest cause of arguments and ultimately break-up for couples. It doesn't help that most couples are financially worse off after breaking up – separation leads to money worries just as money worries lead to separation.

Biblical finances

In biblical terms, socially responsible investing encompasses far more than avoiding your money being used to harm others. Avoiding black-listed companies, such as those that deal in arms or tobacco, damage the environment or exploit workers, is only a first step.[31] Better still is to select companies with positive ethical criteria; those that actively seek to improve life in a particular area.

Without specific training, capital or knowledge, such opportunities may be hard to find. It's unlikely that every criterion can be met all of the time, simply because of the way our economy works. For example, 'social lending networks'[32] offer direct lending facilities, meaning that money can be lent to individuals and groups of individuals for specific purposes. It sounds like a great, relational alternative to the anonymous, responsibility-free choice of banking your cash. However, because these loans typically make their return through payment of interest rather than share of profits, they fail to satisfy the criterion of reaping only where you have sown – an improvement, but not perfect by any means. (One interesting idea would be to try to use such organizations to formalize zero-interest loans between specific individuals, or to encourage borrowers to pay a percentage of profits instead of interest.)

> 'Capitalism wants the biggest cake, socialism is concerned with how the cake is divided, but Christianity is interested in how the cake is made.'   *Paul Williams, economist*

Ordering our finances around relational principles may seem like a lot more responsibility and work. However, we have to remember that this responsibility is warranted: globally speaking we are tremendously privileged to be able to make such financial choices at all. In addition, the alternatives to the (hopefully) beneficial outcomes of managing our money are not morally neutral: we can assume that unless we make positive decisions, the default position will be a harmful one. The capitalist philosophy is that the most profitable option is the best; the Christian approach has to have a higher priority, even if that means lower returns or excluding certain options. Our investment must be used to build relationships with, and benefit, others; the alternative is likely to harm them. We are accountable for what is done with our money, and so should ideally have some influence over how it is used, which also requires transparency. Risk and return should be linked, as the alternative is reaping where we have not sown.

Having said this, the principles offered are not intended to be a series of boxes to tick – which would be impossible for all but a tiny, wealthy and expert minority. In our financial decisions, as in all others, we are encouraged to follow the spirit of the law: justice, fairness, equality and love – not a slavish adherence to the letter.

Meditation

You may say to yourself, 'My power and the strength of my hands have produced this wealth for me.' But remember the LORD your God, for it is he who gives you the ability to produce wealth, and so confirms his covenant, which he swore to your forefathers, as it is today. (Deut. 8.17–18)

Discussion questions

- Identify all the different places you have money (or debt) at the moment – bank accounts, insurance companies, credit cards, savings, pensions, shares and other assets. In each case, why did you choose it, and do you know what your money is being used for?
- What changes could you make to use your money more relationally, and actively, to ensure justice?
- Are there ways in which you could find relational ways of avoiding debt or unnecessary purchase – for example, by pooling or sharing resources?

8

Spiritual health

———•·◆·•———

                              From Yes! *magazine*[1]

Previous chapters have focused on how we act – the external answers we might give in response to various ethical questions posed by the world around us. This chapter looks not just at how we approach our relationships with others, but at the internal relationship each of us has with ourself. This, of course, powerfully influences the nature of our external relationships. How we have been treated in the past, by family, friends and others; what aspects of our personalities have been encouraged or discouraged; questions of self-image and self-esteem; the extent to which we trust others and how we go about getting to know people: all of these affect how we relate to others, and how they in turn relate to us. And although it can be tempting to see our faith as completely separate from these questions, we can't assume that our relationship with God is immune from them. Our understanding of God determines how we act, but is also shaped by our experiences of the world around us.

Consumer Christianity

As informed consumers we make choices every day. We choose which supermarket we go to for our groceries, which chain we prefer for coffee, which companies supply our electricity and gas. If we don't like a TV programme – or perhaps even the adverts in between a programme's segments – then we change the channel. We can hardly be expected to continue to buy a certain brand of toothpaste if we are sceptical about how well it cleans our teeth, or continue to go to the same bakery for lunch when they take our favourite sandwich off the menu. We're good at tuning out of our lives the things that don't suit us. But should the same rules apply to our faith?

For example, many of us are in a position to choose which church we attend, particularly if we live in a big city. Some people spend many weeks 'shopping' for the best experience of 'church', perhaps never properly settling anywhere. But, more dangerously, this con-sumerization of faith – 'consumer Christianity' – is also true of those areas of life where we can't quite see how Christianity is relevant, or where we can't see how God could be active – such as in the case of evil and suffering. If we can't or don't want to engage with it, it's easy to carry over the same approach that we apply to the rest of our lives. This doesn't necessarily mean abandoning our faith altogether – just as we may not completely abandon our usual supermarket just because it fails to stock a few particular items. But it does mean that we are led to deny God's sovereignty and influence over certain areas, which inevitably means we end up looking elsewhere for our source of authority and guidance.

> I always thought that Christianity was a great idea. But I couldn't accept the idea of the resurrection – it just didn't make sense to me scientifically. I thought it was OK to be a Christian and leave that bit out. But eventually I began to realize how important it was. Without the crucifixion and resurrection, there's no solution to sin, no proof of who Jesus really was, or of life after death. And what does your faith really look like without those? John, 39

Treating God the same way we treat our weekly shop won't make for a vibrant faith. The Bible doesn't suggest that we will understand everything that happens to us, or that making the right choices will mean we escape suffering – if anything, the opposite. The Bible doesn't separate faith from the full range of human emotional experience, whether we view it positively or negatively. Contemplating his crucifixion in the Garden of Gethsemane, Jesus 'began to be deeply distressed and troubled. "My soul is overwhelmed with sorrow to the point of death," he said to them' (Mark 14.33–34). And yet this was the culmination of his ministry: however much he did not want this terrible death, 'Yet not what I will, but what you will' (14.36). Suffering was an integral, crucial part of Jesus' journey – as it is for many Christians around the world today.

We are not called to be silent or inarticulate when faced with painful situations. The psalms are full of the authors' very real emotions – joy, fear, anger, hope, bewilderment, dismay. In Psalm 73, Asaph admits to envying the arrogant and resenting his own obedience to God when he sees how easy and prosperous the lives of the wicked are in comparison to his own suffering. Proverbs acknowledges the power of feelings – 'Anger is cruel and fury overwhelming, but who can stand before jealousy?' (27.4) – as well as their complexity: 'Even in laughter the heart may ache, and joy may end in grief' (14.13).

In many cases, this anger and misery occurs not only despite the authors' faith, but *because* of it. Jeremiah was clearly bitterly unhappy with his prophetic call, expressing this repeatedly and at length. Lamentations, a little-read book of the Bible traditionally viewed as being penned by Jeremiah, is a series of mournful poems grieving the destruction of Jerusalem and the state of those who remain alive. Jeremiah's depressive outlook throughout his ministry – before and after the destruction – has prompted the term 'Jeremiad', meaning a long, pessimistic work of criticism towards society. Although God encourages him, corrects him and occasionally even rebukes him for his lack of stamina (Jer. 12.5), he never claims that a life of obedience to him means that such feelings are simply invalid.

> 'The real problem is not why some pious, humble, believing people suffer, but why some do not.'   C. S. Lewis[2]

Consumer Christianity says something like:

> Jesus loves you and wants to bless you. He can take away your problems. He will deal with your depression and anger and frustration, he can give you success at work and answer your prayers for your ambition and hopes for life (provided of course that you're praying in line with his will, which you probably are because he created you and gave you your talents and potential in the first place).

It's a warm, comfortable, reassuring message. Like the best lies, it's close to the truth. But it's not what Jesus says. As consumers, we start with ourselves and ask, 'What can Christianity do for me? How is it worth my effort?' And so often, we are given the answers we want to hear and end up with a safe, tame, Western, middle-class faith that doesn't look much different from anyone else's lives.

'In this world you will have trouble. But take heart! I have overcome the world' (John 16.33). That's what Jesus actually says – not some slick salesman pitch about how he will fit in with our lives and help us fulfil our potential for him, but a warning that the Christian life shouldn't be easy because 'the world' has values that are fundamentally opposed to the kingdom. Our comfort cannot be in material blessings or even emotional well-being, but in our ultimate hope in him. One of the reasons we find our faith challenged in times of suffering is that we've bought into false promises about what following Jesus is really about.

Like the psalms, there are many examples of worship songs and hymns that are full of references to persevering faith in times of trial. The nineteenth-century American lawyer Horatio Spafford wrote the famous hymn, 'It is well with my soul', after a series of tragedies claimed the life of his son, almost everything he owned and then finally the lives of all four of his daughters. More recently, worship leader Matt Redman wrote 'Blessed be your name' against the background of the impact of his father's suicide when he was seven, his wife's suffering three miscarriages and, most specifically, after being in the USA during the terrorist attacks of September 11, 2001. Both of these well-known songs express the truth that God's goodness and sovereignty is absolute, however painful our present circumstances.

The way we approach the rest of life can too easily be extended to our faith: picking and choosing, cutting out those aspects that do not fit with our preconceived ideas and desires. This is not meant to dismiss the pain of the struggles that some people experience. However, there is no sound biblical basis for the common assumption that faith should prevent depression, anxiety or other emotional problems. Consumer Christianity is often threatened by suffering because it's about how God can serve us – if something goes wrong, we assume he's not holding up his end of the deal. But Christians who are trying to remain faithful through suffering can also feel like failures, because the underlying message of consumer Christianity is: 'Jesus will make you happy.' So many Christians experience depression, pain and suffering, and then feel guilty on top of that because they've bought into the idea that Christians shouldn't experience such troubles.

'As yourself . . .'

It's hard for me to believe in a loving father God when my own father was so cold. I had everything I needed materially but I don't think I ever once felt any warmth from him. He just didn't want be around, like I was an inconvenience. Calling God 'Father' has difficult associations for me.

Edward, 28

We also need to remember that there's a closer link between spiritual and emotional health than is often assumed. One of the main points of this book is that our faith isn't a bubble, separate from everything else. Like it or not, it stretches into every area of our lives. Our faith should determine the way we act, but the way we act and react to the world around us also has an impact on our faith – that's why it's so important to make deliberate decisions, rather than go with the flow of a culture that doesn't share Christianity's values.

Cognitive behavioural therapists call this two-way process 'emotional reasoning'. There is some popular understanding of this idea. Someone who sees the world 'through rose-tinted glasses' is a person who's generally inclined to be happy and seems to look on the bright side, able to discount the negative they experience. The point is that the person's naturally happy mood influences their understanding of their world. Similarly, when we are already in a low mood, it's harder to believe that other people or even God mean well for us. Under such circumstances God's promises in the Bible offer a vital anchor for the changeable nature of our faith.

Our experiences of earthly relationships can colour our expectations of our relationship with God, and how we perceive God can have an effect on our own feelings. For example, many people who have lacked a supportive and loving father, for whatever reason, find the image of God as a heavenly father difficult to relate to. Our earthly parents provide our first experiences of both protective love and discipline; if one of these aspects of care has been stressed at the expense of the other we may find our expectations of God similarly coloured. If God is seen primarily as a judge, this can lead to feelings of overwhelming guilt. Conversely, if his mercy is overemphasized this can lead to sin on the grounds that he will always forgive us – something Paul warns against in Romans 3.7–8:

> Someone might argue, 'If my falsehood enhances God's truthfulness and so increases his glory, why am I still condemned as a sinner?' Why not say – as some are being slanderously reported as saying and as some claim that we say – 'Let us do evil that good may result'? Their condemnation is deserved.

In exploring a relational approach to different ethical issues, this book has repeatedly drawn attention to Jesus' summary of the Law in Matthew 22.34–40: 'Love the Lord your God' and 'Love your neighbour as yourself'. While self-love is not a core part of Jesus' summary, like love for God and neighbour, this does presuppose that we have a degree of self-esteem.

This is not the same as self-centredness. Our treatment of others should be healthy and positive, reflecting the way we feel about ourselves as redeemed children of God. It's often the case that those who have little self-esteem find it hard to love others – as they seem unlovable to themselves, it's difficult to believe that others will love them too. Although this is not Jesus' primary message here, 'Love your neighbour as yourself' implies that right relationship with others is helped by correct understanding of, and right relationship with, ourselves: our approach to our 'internal world' is of vital importance to our lives and relationships.

Engaging with culture

This two-way process is also important because it means that what we consume helps to determine our character, as well as vice versa.

That's why Paul writes in Philippians 4.8, 'Whatever is true, whatever is noble, whatever is right, whatever is pure, whatever is lovely, whatever is admirable – if anything is excellent or praiseworthy – think about such things.' When it comes to 'consuming' secular culture, we can often fail to recognize its effects on us. Solomon wrote, 'Above all, guard your heart, for it is the wellspring of life' (Prov. 4.23).

What happens when we allow that wellspring to become contaminated by the less pleasant aspects of consumer entertainment? Inevitably, we end up dissatisfied, because consumerism depends on dissatisfaction – the satisfied consumer is a contradiction, because satisfied consumers no longer *need* to consume. The dissatisfaction might be about our looks (especially if our 'ideal' image comes from magazines and film), how much we earn (thanks to the rise of celebrity culture) or what we own (courtesy of the wing of the advertising industry that equates ownership with identity and personal fulfilment). The result is typically low self-esteem and perhaps high debt. Christians have to be able to critique the culture they consume, because the effects of consumer culture are never neutral. If we can't discern the healthy from the unhealthy, we will be dissatisfied and miserable almost by default.

Writing about the way Christians fail to critique the films they watch, one historian states:

> The respected British director David Puttnam expresses a wide-spread feeling: 'Movies now have an underlying nastiness in them. The thing I loathe more than anything has become fashionable – cynicism.' The irony is that as cinema has become more violent and sexually explicit, Christians have become more relaxed about it. Evangelicals, for example, will happily watch films that would have shocked an earlier generation. As one scholar puts it, contemporary evangelicals are 'comfortable in the world' and 'take for granted many of the cultural norms of middle-class life'. Cinema is lapped up as a form of entertainment, and there is often a lack of critical engagement with the medium or the message. If the danger in the past was cultural separatism, the danger today may be cultural assimilation.[3]

We have not guarded our hearts. Our entertainment habits are another area in which Christians show little difference from our surrounding culture – something that must have an impact on our character and therefore feeds back into the way we approach the world. And as in the other areas explored in this book, the solution is not to withdraw – not to avoid film and TV or to take a simplistic approach by, say, avoiding anything with an '18' certificate – but to engage carefully and judiciously. This means doing more than counting up the occurrences of swearing, violence and nudity and making a recommendation based on the total, as some independent classification groups do:

> The US-based Christian Film and Television Commission also placed an extreme caution warning against *Schindler's List* because of the 'extensive nudity in concentration camp scenes . . . graphic sex scenes between unmarried individuals . . . [and] 19 obscenities, 8 profanities and several vulgarities'. Faced with one of the great moral evils of our century, these reviewers could do little more than tot up the number of swear words.[4]

This is not to say that we should ignore these elements, only that the value of a film does not begin and end with them. Engaging with film, TV and our broader culture in any area means more than either unthinking acceptance or shocked, reactionary rejection. It means making considered, deliberate responses that both reflect and reinforce our Christian identities and values.

Different how?

Putting relationships first – both our relationships with God and with other people – may mean radically shifting our priorities. It's not just a philosophical idea or an intellectual value: it will change the shape of our lives in every area. These are not easy questions; we do not live in an ideal world, and there are few simple answers. For example, do we work long hours, including weekends, or do we accept less pay for fewer hours of work, perhaps giving up opportunities for promotion, in order to spend more time with our family and friends – and where do we draw the line? Do we move house or job or both, and risk leaving our existing networks of relationships behind, or do we make staying in the same place an option in the interests of maintaining them, even if it costs us in other ways?

What about the relationships we have with people we will never meet? This means the ones who are affected by our spending and living habits, whether because they are involved in the production of what we use or because our actions have an effect on the environment in which they live. Is out of sight really out of mind, or do we take responsibility for how our choices make a difference, whether positive or negative, to their lives?

In terms of ourselves, is our self-esteem based on how we look and how much we earn – in absolute or relative terms – or on *who* we know and how we relate to them? Are our identities found in what we buy or desire to possess, or the relationships we cultivate at home, work, church and elsewhere? What do we see when we look in the mirror: a person made in the image of God or a reflection of the values of consumer magazines and TV?

And what about the relationships themselves? Do we treat them in a consumeristic way? Are our relationships – with partners, friends, family, colleagues – essentially seen as disposable, worth pursuing for as long as they serve our ends and satisfy us, or are we willing to deal with difficulties and make sacrifices in the interests of sustaining relationships over the long term?

In practice, this might mean turning down a higher paid job in another town because it would mean relocating away from friends and relatives, or at least commuting long hours, leaving less time for family. It will probably mean sticking with 'difficult' people through their problems, even when our instincts are to distance ourselves from them. It might mean holding on through a rocky period in a marriage or relationship with a boyfriend or girlfriend, rather than choosing to break up because that is the easiest solution at the time. It will mean making a conscious effort to put in extra time and effort to maintain existing relationships that perhaps we've drifted away from because one or other of our circumstances has changed. In church, it means being sacrificially inclusive of people we might never choose to spend time with otherwise – exercising the *agape*, or unconditional love, that Jesus said would be the hallmark of Christians: 'A new command I give you: Love one another. As I have loved you, so you must love one another. By this all men will know that you are my disciples, if you love one another' (John 13.34–35).

There is an echo of the uncomfortable line in the Lord's Prayer here, 'Forgive us our debts, as we also have forgiven our debtors.' Both imply that our grateful response to God's own forgiveness and love for us must be to extend them to others. Inevitably, adopting the values of consumerism affects our relationships with God. If we are accustomed to picking and choosing the relationships that work best for us, the assumption is that others do the same too. If that's just how relationships work in our worldview, do we really believe that God is any different? And although God's love for us is unconditional, it is not his will that the love we extend to others has conditions to it. '*As I have loved you*, so you must love one another.'

'*St Peter, don't you call me 'cause I can't go;*
I owe my soul to the company store.'

Merle Travis, 'Sixteen Tons'

Consumerism tells us that relationships are great so long as the other person fulfils our needs in some way. So long as they don't become too boring, too annoying, too much hard work in some way – fine. When they do, it's our right to find a better match for our needs. But that's not the only way it affects the way we approach our faith. The first commandment states, 'You shall have no other gods before me.' When possessions and desire compete for our loyalty it affects our ability to serve God. But also, in the effects it has on the way we structure our lives, consumerism is intensely damaging to a Christian faith. When life is a 24/7 hurry – to work, to achieve, to use our time actively and 'constructively' in our jobs or leisure – time spent with God, at church and in fellowship with other Christians, can become marginalized. In the same way, when there are so many pressures on our finances, giving can easily be squeezed out.

These aspects of faith can so often become no more than add-ons to the rest of our hectic lives. In fact, our busyness can perversely be seen as the means by which we honour God. As one critic notes:

The pitiable religious consumerist thinks if he just works harder he will be able 'to make time' for God and others, but he is afraid that any 'slacking off' [of] his hectic schedule is a failure to use God's gifts in providing for the self-fulfilment of his family. By some demonic alchemy, love of God has come to mean giving thanks for His gifts by maximizing productive 'self-actualization' while love of neighbor has come to mean providing them with consumer goods. One need only examine the finances of a typical Christian family in America during the aftermath of Christmas to see how pervasive this mentality has become.[5]

Purposeful living

Rather than allow these things to be after-thoughts, when we make conscious decisions about the way we spend our time and money we should remember that they have implications for the way we then structure the rest of our lives. God calls for our best: Cain's sin in Genesis 4.3 was not that he gave nothing but that he gave no special thought to his offering, whereas Abel gave the best portions of the firstborn of his flock. If we believe that a financial commitment to a church or charity is worthwhile, then making it a priority will have knock-on effects for the way we can use the rest of our money. We may find we need to make changes – even painful ones – to our spending in other areas. However, this kind of deliberate management of our budget is a powerful antidote to a consumerist mentality because it forces us to be intentional about the way we live, rather than be swept along by the prevailing values by default and fit in our faith around the edges. Similarly, when we ring-fence time commitments such as taking Sundays off, setting aside time for worship, friends, family and fellowship, we intentionally and fundamentally ground our lives on something more than the drive for acquisition. It is a reminder that our time and money are not our own; they are just temporary gifts from God.

> Over the last two years I've seen most of my closest friends move away – some a few miles, some to other towns. I really feel that God has placed community on my heart, for the church and outside of it, and I thought that we were beginning to create that. But it's so hard when others don't share your vision and passion for that. For them, it's nice while it lasts, but it's not a good enough reason to stay. Sarah, 35

This may be frustrating for people who would love to live at a slower pace and would value more time to spend with friends and family, but who are prevented by circumstances apparently beyond their control (including the amount of time everyone else has free to spend with them). To reiterate what was said above: these are not easy questions and we do not live in an ideal world. But each one of us will, at some point, look back on our lives and ask whether we would have done things differently, at whatever cost. We will each leave a legacy, and the nature of that legacy will depend on the principles by which we lived.

> Good personal relationships distinguish the impression you leave behind in this world. It was said that the pollster George Gallup had written on his tombstone, '84 per cent of people think I have gone to heaven.' It's more likely someone will be remembered as 'A beloved son and father' than as 'The executive who restructured his company three times in five years and thus sustained shareholder value through a difficult period in the markets'.[6]

Dual citizens

For Christians, living as 'dual citizens' of the kingdom of God and our secular society,[7] there is constant competition for our identities and for the guiding principles and ideologies by which we live our lives. Our culture is one suffused with consumerism, and its messages of individualism, ownership, desire and intrinsic dissatisfaction are fundamentally opposed to the Christian one of outward-looking right relationship, with God and with other people, as the means by which we find our identities and understand our place in the world. What we consume from the culture around us is of vital importance in determining that identity, and cannot be neatly separated from the kind of people we are – or can expect to become. That kind of compartmentalization is unrealistic because it suggests that we can place areas of our lives outside of God's sovereignty but expect this to have no impact on our relationship with him, or on the rest of our lives.

Our citizenship is in heaven (Phil. 3.20). This does not mean we should resign ourselves to being strangers in a hostile world. Instead we should actively be bringing the values of the kingdom to the place in which we currently live, changing it as best we can rather than waiting out our time here and merely trying to avoid the worst of it – or worse, failing to make any real distinction. We have lost the Israelites' idea of 'holiness' as separation from their surrounding religious and cultural influences – not primarily in terms of with-drawal and isolation, but in terms of remaining distinctive in the areas that really matter. The Israelites weren't commanded to avoid any contact with foreign cultures, only to take care not to adopt practices that risked compromising their own religious identity. For modern Christians, by drawing such clear boundaries we ground our existence and identity in something stable, rather than in the endless quest to acquire and experience something more just to stay as happy as we are now – the 'hedonic treadmill'. Many such challenges and contributors to our identities arise every day. Some will go unnoticed as they are so taken for granted against the background of our normal cultural expectations. Others we may be dimly aware of, and perhaps only a few will register as real threats or opportunities to us. Character-forming events are often presented as rare occasions – a time when there is a significant decision to be made, a clear choice between right and wrong. But this ignores the soil out of which they grow: the history of the hundreds of minor decisions we take every day that make up our habits and the kind of person we are, and therefore the path we are most likely to take when we finally reach those major events, like a journey that becomes automatic through long familiarity or a recipe book that falls open at a particular page from repeated consultation for a favourite dish. Jesus said, 'Make a tree good and its fruit will be good' (Matt. 12.33); it is those habits that gradually bring about this change. Perhaps all that really happens in character-forming events is a moment of self-realization – the knowledge of what we have slowly been growing into all this time. The competition for our characters and lives is determined not primarily by the infrequent decisions we are forced to make, but in the myriad examples of how we choose to act and what we choose to be every day.

Meditation

> God has said, 'Never will I leave you; never will I forsake you.' So we say with confidence, 'The Lord is my helper; I will not be afraid. What can man do to me?'   (Heb. 13.5–6)

Discussion questions

- What do you think are the main messages that consumer culture sends us?
- What are the characteristics of God's love for you? How can you show similar qualities in particular relationships in your life?
- Write a list of the things that you think define you, and their relative importance – for example, work, friends, possessions, faith.

Write a second list of the things that you would like to define you. Is there a gap between the two, and if so, what practical steps can you take to get from the first to the second?

- What are your major questions or doubts about Christianity, and how do these affect your faith on a day-to-day level?

9

Conclusion: whole-life discipleship

———◆•◆•◆———

Consumer culture tells us that life is all about choice – the more the better. That way I'll be able to find something to fit my wants and needs. While that sounds great in theory, in practice the 'me-centred' culture is isolating and lonely. Happiness is only ever a choice away, but somehow it always seems to be the next choice, not the one you just made. Something is always missing.

Christianity tells us that life isn't about the range of choices on offer, and not about 'me' at all – at least not on my own. 'Me' is only ever one half of a relationship. We've been looking at what's missing from consumer culture, namely the *other* half. It's not about legalism, pages of instructions and checklists. It's about showing love for God and neighbour in everything we do. Maybe that's not as easy as legalism, but it's certainly more effective and pleasing to God.

Navigating the maze of choices on offer – 'ethical' or otherwise – must be more than a matter of blunt rules. Modelling faith through all our relationships in a whole-life, deliberate way cannot be reduced to ticking boxes. Faced with the desire to live a 'good' or 'ethical' lifestyle, we risk making the same mistake as the Pharisees Jesus criticizes in the New Testament.

Instead, when we look at the different ethical choices we make, there are a number of questions we might ask ourselves. What do we actually hope to achieve through this transaction – whether it is an emotional exchange, a financial one or otherwise? What are the reasons and principles that lie behind our decisions? Are we trying to maximize value-for-money or personal pleasure, or to affirm ourselves – whether in the food we buy, the bank account we use or the way we spend our time? In each instance, what realistically is the deciding factor – what is the one aspect that is non-negotiable and takes precedence over all else? For the Christian, the same question could be stated as, 'Who is your God?' If each decision is reduced to that one simple test, without any complicating factors, we might be surprised by some of our answers.

But putting God first doesn't trivialize everything else. In fact even the most trivial-seeming things take on a new importance when God takes his rightful place in our lives, because nothing – no area of life, no situation, no relationship – is outside of his will for us.

> 'It's not the case that God matters more than everything else, so nothing else matters in the light of him. On the contrary: because God matters infinitely, everything else matters much more in the light of him.
>
> So the environment matters immensely, because God is Creator of the world. He loves his world, is committed to it, died for it, and will ultimately re-create it. Art matters because we're made in God's image, and his creativity has been passed on to us. Justice matters, because it's an intrinsic component of God's character. That's why Christians are to be at the forefront of shaping and contributing to issues of the environment, the arts, and justice, as we seek to witness to our Creator and bring glory to him.
>
> Simon Guillebaud, missionary and writer[1]

This book is also meant as a challenge to our churches to be different from the surrounding culture and to show their faith throughout what they practise, in addition to what they preach. Quite simply, it is contradictory to run events and services to win people to Christ and bring them to a deeper faith if, in the process, we are feeding them with rice grown with child labour so that we can entertain them cheaply; seating them on chairs made from non-renewable wood that incentivizes deforestation and the destruction of the natural habitats that God created; sheltering them in buildings mortgaged to banks that make their money by investing in tobacco, arms and pornography, exploiting low-income countries or through complex derivatives that harm the economy instead of benefiting others; and making sure the floors and surfaces are clean for them by hiring someone on the minimum wage to come in because we don't have enough of a sense of community for church members to organize a rota to do it themselves.

We need to broaden our ideas about how we shape the communities in which we live. How we act, the organizations we get involved in, where we shop, who we hold to account; all the relationships we form and cultivate – these have an enormous impact on the kind of society of which we are a part. Although there are always going to be factors beyond our control, it's only by engaging that we're going to change our environment. That means living by the kind of values we would like to see in our own community. It's inconsistent to complain that the friendly, local shops are disappearing if we're a part of the problem because we always go to the out-of-town supermarkets ourselves, or to campaign for the release from debt of low-income countries when the rate of interest on our savings and value of shares in our pensions depends on it. The popular challenge when people complain about one or other aspect of government policy is, 'Did you vote?' – the rationale supposedly being that if you voted a party in, or didn't bother to go to the polls against them, you hardly have a right to grumble about what they are doing with your consent. But our say is not restricted to a ballot box every few years. Every time we buy or do not buy, drive or walk, turn the heating up or pull on a jumper, take any one of the myriad choices we face every day, we are in some sense voting for the future of ourselves and of many other people as well.

Some of these choices have clear and immediate implications; others have no visible result and will not unless many other people do the same. For example, taking a job near to home rather than accepting an hour's commute each way will have all kinds of immediate consequences – more time with friends and family, a different set of co-workers, probably different pay and more opportunities to become involved with the local community in various ways. Changing your bank because you are dissatisfied with its ethical policy may make some difference to your balance, but it's unlikely to result in a change to the company's practices unless thousands of others also make a stand. The same is true of shopping: your individual choice to buy products that embody a particular set of values will not make much difference to the producer or environment if you are the only one making that choice.

However, this spectrum of consequences, from the measurable to the invisible, is misleading for several reasons. The extreme form of this results in a mindset that would make no decisions based on anything other than self-interest: unless we see a clear benefit to ourselves, there is no point in doing it. As we have argued throughout this book, an individualistic mindset is intensely damaging to ourselves, our closest relationships and to society as a whole. It assumes that each of us is the centre of his or her universe, and exists in a vacuum in which our choices affect no one else, and the choices of others have no effect on us. In reality we are part of a complex network of relationships, and our lives are impacted on by people we do not know just as much as our individual decisions have consequences for those we may never meet. Whether or not we accept it, we are responsible for the outcomes our lifestyles have at the other end of the supply chain and beyond: financial, environmental, relational and emotional. In any case, such decisions are rarely taken alone. Political disillusionment and apathy might be running at an all-time high, but consumer power remains strong. When people vote with their money in sufficient numbers, corporations tend to take notice. Examples range from the early abolitionists' boycott of sugar grown with slave labour, to the partial success of the Nestlé boycott in protest against the company's aggressive promotion of formula milk over breast milk in low-income countries.

The final reason to make these small but significant choices is because they are habit-forming and therefore character-forming. The Bible draws little distinction between visible actions of injustice, such as robbery or financial oppression, and those that are carried out in secret, such as adultery and idolatry (Ezek. 18). 'Public' and 'private' injustice are treated the same because they are both different expressions of the same core character and attitude towards God and others. Pretending we can compartmentalize life so neatly is an act of self-delusion. Who we are – our character – is as much the result of the mosaic of choices we make every day as it is the cause of those decisions. 'Make a tree good and its fruit will be good, or make a tree bad and its fruit will be bad, for a tree is recognized by its fruit . . . out of the overflow of the heart the mouth speaks' (Matt. 12.33–34). This is what a 'Jubilee lifestyle' or being 'free to live' looks like: the complete integration of our faith with the everyday choices we make, the same character evident in the big decisions as the small ones, whether public or private. The psalmist summarizes so well the basis as well as the reward of such a lifestyle:

> '*Commit your way to the LORD;*
>   *trust in him and he will do this:*
> *He will make your righteousness shine like the dawn,*
>   *the justice of your cause like the noonday sun.*'
>   *Psalm 37.6*

Appendix 1
Background to the financial crisis

A recession is when your neighbour loses his job. A depression is when you lose yours. Attributed to Dave Beck, US labour leader, 1954

On the surface, the causes of the credit crunch and recession are now fairly clear, even if there is still debate about how much blame should be attributed to each cause. With hindsight, the effects of these cultural, economic and technological changes unfolded like clockwork into what became known as the Global Financial Crisis, an economic disaster seemingly far greater than the sum of its parts. These are the details to which the analysts and policy-makers cling; if we know what went wrong, goes the argument, we can prevent it from happening again.

> **Recession**
> Strictly speaking, a recession is defined as two consecutive quarters of negative growth in an economy. In other words, over two three-month periods, the total value of all the goods and services sold by a country decreases. This can be quite a clumsy measure of recession, which is more generally understood as a slowdown after a peak of activity in businesses and services. It usually lasts at least several months. Personal income falls and unemployment rises.

After the last major recession at the beginning of the 1990s, the second half of that decade saw a sustained period of economic growth in the West, and particularly in the USA. There was low unemployment and a boom in the technology sector as the rise of the internet offered businesses and investors new opportunities. By early 2000, however, it was clear that the 'dot-com bubble' could not go on for ever. Investors had been buying stocks in technology companies simply because they expected them to continue increasing in value, not because they were intrinsically worth anything. In addition, thanks to the 'Y2K' or 'millennium-bug' scare, by this stage companies had already bought all the computer equipment they would need for the immediate future. Realizing their shares were overvalued, some investors started to sell, and falling prices then caused others to follow suit in panic. The market crashed: the NASDAQ – a stock market index that includes a large number of technology companies – fell by around three-quarters over the next three years.

A brief, mild recession followed in the USA in 2001 (recovery occurred quickly but was slowed by the terrorist attacks of September 11). This, along with new technology and the deregulation of the world's financial systems that had been occurring since the 1970s (particularly in the 1980s in the UK, under Margaret Thatcher), paved the way for the next boom and bust.

By the end of 2001, interest rates had been cut sharply to help bring the USA out of recession, meaning that it was cheap to borrow money. People could buy houses they could not have afforded two years earlier. The lack of banking regulation multiplied risks. Banks and mortgage companies – encouraged in part by government policy and popular desire for home ownership – gave mortgages to people who, under other conditions, wouldn't have been able to pay for them. Investors who had lost faith in the stock market after the dot-com crash also turned to property. House prices were rising all the time thanks to the flood of new investors, so banks continued to lend and customers continued to apply for new mortgages, believing they couldn't lose. The new homeowners also borrowed against the value of their houses, taking out extra debt on the grounds that the rising prices of the assets they owned would be able to pay for it.

Many of the new mortgagees had bad credit histories, but if their 'sub-prime' customers defaulted, the banks assumed that the houses they repossessed would easily pay for the debt. So the banks also believed that the investments they had made were safe.

Rather than hold the mortgage investments themselves, banks and other lenders bundled together the loans they had made into 'mortgage-backed securities'. These packages of smaller loans could then be sold on to outside investors, who would collect the mortgage repayments and take possession of the houses in the event of default. The companies could then lend out the money they raised for new mortgages. The higher the risk of default on these packages of mortgages, the higher the potential returns. The problem was that their true level of risk wasn't properly established when the mortgage-backed securities were bought by investment banks, because it was based on the previous years of rising property prices, and because the riskiness of the individual mortgages that made them up was not examined.

In June 2004, the US Federal Reserve began the first of a series of interest-rate rises to combat inflation. Over two years, rates were raised from 1 per cent to 5.25 per cent. The low interest rates that had enabled many people to buy their homes were suddenly a thing of the past. Property values, which were expected to continue rising indefinitely, peaked in 2005 – demand had decreased because fewer people could afford to buy. Homeowners began to default on their mortgages, and house prices started to fall in 2006.

Inflation is the change over time in how much your money can buy – effectively how much it's worth. For example, if your total monthly spending – rent, bills, food, travel, entertainment – amounts to £1,000 in a month one year, and purchasing exactly the same things that month one year later costs £1,050, then the value of your money has gone down; inflation in this case is 5 per cent, because your total purchases are 5 per cent more expensive than they were last year. Unless your income is also greater, it will be harder to buy the same things (which is why yearly pay often increases with inflation).

Deflation is when your money can buy more than it could previously, because for one reason or another things are cheaper (oil or food prices have come down, technology is cheaper, etc). While this sounds like a good thing, if people know that prices are heading downwards, they tend not to spend as much because they know they will be able to buy things more cheaply in the future. That means that shops and businesses suffer and jobs may be lost as a result.

Mortgage lenders suddenly realized they were in trouble. The investment banks around the world, which had bought mortgage-backed securities worth billions of dollars, also found that the assets they'd

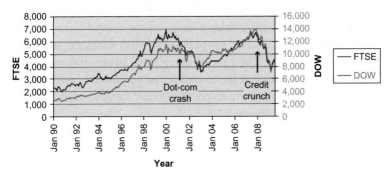

Figure 1 FTSE/Dow Jones stock indices
Source: Historical data from <http://uk.finance.yahoo.com>.

purchased were worth far less than they expected. Their profits dropped sharply. Bad results from one bank, BNP Paribas, on 9 August 2007, prompted the first of a series of heavy falls on the world's stock markets, as global investors realized that their shares in these banks would turn out to be worth less than they thought – see Figure 1.

> 'At this juncture, the impact on the broader economy and financial markets of the problems in the subprime market seems likely to be contained.'
>
> *Ben Bernanke, Federal Reserve chairman, March 2007*

Because banks had bought 'packages' of mortgages, without scrutinizing each individual mortgage, they didn't know how much their investments were worth. They were uncertain how much money they owned, and became unwilling to lend it out to each other. The amount of credit they made available to each other shrank to almost zero – the credit crunch. Central banks around the world made loans to their countries' commercial banks to encourage them to lend, but this didn't help as much as hoped – partly because it was still uncertain who would be able to pay them back. In September 2007, the UK bank Northern Rock had to ask the Bank of England for a loan to help continue run its business. Northern Rock had borrowed heavily from other banks to fund its mortgage lending, rather than use mainly savers' money. Now that the other banks weren't lending freely, depositors in the bank feared that its business would collapse, taking their money down with it, and withdrew £1 billion in just one day from their accounts. Northern Rock was fully nationalized in February 2008, to save it from failing entirely and to ensure that the money it had borrowed from the Bank of England – effectively the taxpayer – would be paid back.

In late 2007 and through 2008, the scale of the losses to banks and other financial institutions emerged, prompting further stock-market falls. The problems were now filtering through to the 'real economy', meaning they were not just affecting the financial sector but other companies too. As banks were reluctant to lend money, many businesses found it difficult to stay afloat. Reduced profit, redundancies and falling share prices followed. Rising unemployment and hard-to-obtain mortgages meant fewer buyers, and house prices fell in both the USA and the UK. At the same time inflation was also increasing. This was partly a consequence of the same factors that had led to the credit crunch: the creation of so much debt meant extra purchasing power, hence a high worldwide demand for limited resources. Inflation rose to over 5 per cent in July, as oil reached almost $150 per barrel and food prices rose due to poor harvests. Some economists suggested that speculators had turned to oil, grain and other commodities instead of shares, pushing prices up further – the 'commodities bubble'. Inflation put further pressure on businesses and consumers in the UK.

> 'Lehman have changed their recommendation on Lehman from "hold" to "sell" . . .'
> *Anon.*

In September 2008 the global investment bank Lehman Brothers filed for bankruptcy – the largest bankruptcy in US history. The same week, the US Federal Reserve bought an 80 per cent share of the insurance giant American International Group for $85 billion. AIG was judged 'too important to fail' as the consequences to the financial organizations it had insured would have been catastrophic for the global economy. The amount given to bail out AIG was eventually doubled to $170 billion.

In the UK, rumours of difficulties caused the value of shares of the banking group HBOS to fluctuate wildly. Economists and politicians criticized the traders they suspected of spreading these rumours in order to profit from short selling HBOS stock. Soon afterwards it was confirmed that Lloyds TSB would buy the bank. On 19 September the Financial Services Authority banned some short selling, which it believed at the time may have led to HBOS's devaluation and subsequent takeover.

Short selling

Short selling is a way of making money from shares going down in price, rather than the more common way of profiting from an increase in share value. A company (often a hedge fund) or individual effectively borrows shares from someone else and sells them in the hope that the price will drop. Then they can buy the same number of shares at a cheaper price, give them back to the original owner and keep the difference. It's a bit like borrowing a coat from a friend, taking it back to the shop for a refund, then buying the same coat in the sales for less money, returning it to your friend and keeping the difference in price.

At the end of September, the US House of Representatives rejected the government's $700 billion rescue plan for the US economy, resulting in a record one-day points fall (777 points, 7 per cent) in the Dow Jones.

In October 2008, the Bank of England began the first of five consecutive monthly interest-rate cuts. Rates had been raised as high as 5.75 per cent in July 2007 to try to lower inflation. In October they were reduced from 5 per cent to 4.5 per cent, and by March 2009 rates would be cut to 0.5 per cent. The UK government announced its plans to spend billions of pounds of taxpayers' money to keep the country's largest banks in business. Later in the year, sterling and dollar exchange rates against the euro sank as the low interest rates and bad outlook for the US and UK economies made them unattractive to foreign investors. In the USA, interest rates had been decreasing since late in 2007, and were effectively cut to zero in December 2008 – see Figure 2, overleaf.

Early in 2009 there was a series of UK high-street business failures, very notably Woolworths, as consumer confidence was hit by rising

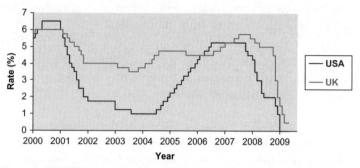

Figure 2 US/UK interest rates 2000–09

unemployment and falling house prices. The recession was made official on 23 January, and was expected to last for most of 2009, unemployment being expected to reach three million.[1] Deflation, instead of inflation, was now the risk for the economy. Across the Atlantic, economists had announced three months earlier, in December 2008, that the recession was official, and had started a year earlier in December 2007. In March, when interest rates had been cut almost to zero without the desired effect, the UK government announced it would begin the process of 'quantitative easing' to provide credit for businesses and individuals.

Quantitative easing

If consumers are not spending enough, businesses struggle and employees lose their jobs. Prices go down to encourage people to buy more products and services, which leads to deflation. Cutting interest rates can help stimulate the economy, because people tend to spend more when it's cheap to borrow money and they will not get much of a return for saving.

If interest-rate cuts don't work, quantitative easing can be another way of raising the amount of money being lent out by banks, and therefore spent by the rest of us. The Bank of England buys assets like government and corporate bonds using money it's effectively created out of nothing. That means that banks and other institutions selling them have more money to lend out. One danger is that the Central Bank creates too much extra money, which devalues the currency and leads to higher inflation than was intended. It is also uncertain just how effective quantitative easing really is in practice. It can also have the effect of undermining exchange rates as foreign investors withdraw their money in the devaluing currency.

At the beginning of April, the leaders of the world's 20 largest economies met in London at the G20 Summit to try to reach an agreement about how to lift the world out of recession. The meetings were accompanied by anti-war, anti-capitalist and environmental protests.

Appendix 2
The complexities of Fairtrade

Although several of the 'labels' mentioned in Chapter 5 – Organic, Local, GM-free – could be critiqued at length, this appendix examines the extent of the issues' complexity by focusing on Fairtrade. The space spent unpacking some of arguments around Fairtrade is not intended to imply that it has not made a valuable contribution to consumer awareness of trade-justice issues, or that it is worse than any other label, only that the problems of ethical shopping are not amenable to a quick fix and have to be viewed in a wider context.

Fairtrade: pros and cons

Fairtrade undoubtedly helps the producer by offering a higher price for produce than the market average by bypassing intermediaries – although in the case of coffee the minimum price set by the Fairtrade Foundation[1] is still lower than historical prices. The Fairtrade brand also raises consumers' general awareness of trade issues. However, Fairtrade remains an inefficient way to help the producer because such a large proportion of the mark-up goes to the retailer and/or to support the Fairtrade brand. There is a danger that Fairtrade can be seen as the only way to trade fairly, which is certainly not the case. There are many different schemes, which have various aims and emphases. In addition, Fairtrade has been criticized on a number of other counts:

Supply and demand

When production outstrips demand, as is currently the case with coffee, market prices are low. Helping a small number of growers by offering them a higher price does not address that underlying problem of overproduction. Some economists have argued that subsidizing some growers makes the others worse off by driving down the price of non-Fairtrade produce; higher prices encourage greater production. Fairtrade addresses this argument by noting that farmers only sell a proportion of their coffee to Fairtrade purchasers, and so it makes no sense for them to increase production, only to sell the majority of their produce at low prices. All the same, the amount of Fairtrade coffee supplied is far greater than demand; the majority of Fairtrade-certified coffee is actually sold to traders at market prices.[2]

Cost

Certification is given after inspection, and the costs are borne by the producer. The daily inspection fee is €400, and initial inspections take several days for smaller producers, up to several weeks for larger plantations, plus additional fees.[3] Although part of these expenses may be covered in some cases by the EU, and there is a 35 per cent discount for small co-operatives of under 50 members, these can still find the entry and annual recertification fees prohibitively expensive.

Investment

To be Fairtrade-registered, producers must be 100 per cent co-operative, all members having equal shares and each having a vote to determine how the money is used. The minimum price greatly benefits these co-operatives. The problem is that co-ops are not the only way that goods are produced. Family-owned farms are not eligible for certification, neither are standalone farms such as many of those in tribal areas of Africa – no matter how poor their owners.

Because every member has an equal share in the co-operative, investment is discouraged because an investor who brings new money or machinery to the co-operative would want a larger share of the profits – which would mean losing the certification. Few coffee farmers work this way in Africa. As one coffee trader commented:

> This structure is now rare in Africa, so only about 2 per cent of all coffee produced can be bought as Fairtrade. Hence, a company like ours could not operate or make much of an impact in Africa if we limited ourselves only to Fairtrade coffees. By defining the moral high ground, and then defining who can stand on it, Fairtrade have left themselves isolated. If as an investor in Africa, I put money in to improve quality, and give the farmers a share in my enterprise, no matter how well I treat them, how much I pay them (even if I pay

them double the Fairtrade price, which is sometimes the case), even if I offer them free health insurance, or build them schools (all things that we are involved in), we cannot and will never be able to have a Fairtrade label, nor will 95 per cent of our suppliers.[4]

The requirements of the Fairtrade certification effectively means that we, in the West, assume we know the best way for African farmers to run their own businesses.

Quality

Organizing farmers into co-operatives discourages investment and discourages quality. Farmers often sell both in Fairtrade and open markets. While the price they receive in the open market is dependent on quality, the price they receive from the Fairtrade market is fixed whatever the quality. So high-quality coffee beans may be sold for a good price on the open market and the remaining beans sold on the Fairtrade market. Because co-operatives mix beans from all their farmers, those farmers who work to improve their quality receive no bonus for doing so, discouraging them from making the effort. Inefficient and low-quality producers are artificially kept in the market.

Together, critics argue, these factors prevent progress, keeping farmers in their current state, preserving current practices rather than encouraging producers out of, say, a foundering industry.

Deeper problems

Trade tariffs prevent exporting countries from gaining the full benefits of their produce, because typically the more refined a product is, the higher the export tariff. For example, 90 per cent of cocoa is produced by low-income countries, but only 4 per cent of chocolate. In addition, local inefficiencies in government, or corruption, can mean that profits are wasted in transport costs, processing fees or payoffs. As one critic notes:

> Farmers I interviewed in Kenya told me that the problems they face are not caused by global influences but their own government's interference. They are forced to use milling companies granted regional monopolies, who fleece them. They want to boost productivity by using fertilizer, but they cannot afford the inflated prices demanded by the

government fertilizer monopoly. Imported tools and machinery would transform their output but are subject to punitive tariffs. Police road-blocks slow their goods and involve money exchanging hands.[5]

Still more fundamentally, although demand for coffee drinks – lattes, Americanos and mint mocha-chip frappuccinos – has never been higher, the reverse is true of green coffee beans. As more coffee producers enter the market and existing ones increase their output, supply has increased even faster than demand. The excess coffee supply has driven down the market price: in 2001, coffee prices in real terms fell to their lowest level ever – largely a result of rapid expansion of production in Brazil and Vietnam. A drop in price can have a devastating effect for entire countries: 'coffee provides 76 per cent of export revenue for Burundi, 68 per cent for Ethiopia, 62 per cent for Rwanda, and 60 per cent for Uganda'.[6] The welfare of whole communities can depend on coffee production and prices.

There are two answers to this: increase demand or decrease supply. We in the West have (despite the recent downturn) enjoyed a period of high economic growth in the last few decades and can afford more luxuries than ever before. But coffee has a low 'income elasticity': there is a limit to the amount of coffee that consumers drink, and unlike, for example, exotic holidays and consumer electronics, an increase in our income does not lead to a corresponding increase in demand for coffee. Overall demand has increased slightly recently, and may continue to do so for a while as emerging economies such as China, India and Russia consume more coffee, but not enough to absorb increases in supply.

The alternative is to reduce supply, thereby raising prices for the remaining growers.

So it would seem that the best coffee to buy are the brands that either pay a high price for a high-quality product, and/or use their profits to incentivize and enable producers to farm something other than coffee, or even to move into non-agricultural employment.

While there are many positive aspects to Fairtrade – offering producers a fair price, developing long-term relationships with them, offering technical support, facilitating social projects such as schools and healthcare and avoiding child labour – we risk missing the best in favour of the good. We would not deny the benefits of any of these aspects, but they are all short-term solutions to an ongoing and larger problem. Encouraging these in the process, a broader solution must be to campaign for the removal of trade barriers, and to incentivize farmers not to grow produce for which there is already a saturated market, like coffee: to help them to diversify, improve quality, or to move into non-agricultural employment.

The challenge for consumers is to recognize that *no* label is a panacea for trade injustice. Ethical shopping is not a matter of ticking the right box and then assuming our choices have no harmful effect on the lives of others.

Notes

Introduction

1 Michael Schluter and John Ashcroft (eds), *Jubilee Manifesto: A framework, Agenda and Strategy for Christian Social Reform* (Leicester: Inter-Varsity Press, 2005).

1 Free to live

1 Cf. e.g. 'Recession almost at an end' in the *Daily Telegraph*, 24 August 2009. See <http://www.telegraph.co.uk/finance/financetopics/recession/6078020/Recession-almost-at-an-end.html>.

2 *The Times*, 'Credit crunch raises divorce rate for America's superwealthy', 11 July 2008.

3 See 'Consumerism' in Graham Cray, *Disciples and Citizens* (Nottingham: Inter-Varsity Press, 2007), pp. 68–80. Note that 'consumerism' has come to mean something similar to 'materialism', but the term originally applied to protecting the rights of purchasers.

4 Cray, *Disciples and Citizens*, p. 68.

5 Quoted in 'The Pope Thinks Young in Australia' in *Time*, 17 July 2008. See <http://www.time.com/time/world/article/0,8599,1823802,00.html>.

6 *The Guardian*, 'Middle-class life and debt, even on a good salary', 4 October 2009.

7 Cray, *Disciples and Citizens*, p. 68.

2 Expressing the love of Christ in an age of debt

1 Terry Pratchett and Neil Gaiman, *Good Omens* (London: Gollancz, 1990), p. 17.

2 Dale Kuehne, *Sex and the iWorld: Rethinking Relationship Beyond an Age of Individualism* (Grand Rapids: Baker Academic, 2009), p. 115.

3 Personal exchange during an Alpha course.

4 Talmud tractate *Shabbat*, 31a.

5 Cf. J. Cheryl Exum and H. G. M. Williamson (eds), *Reading from Right to Left: Essays on the Hebrew Bible in Honour of David J. A. Clines*, JSOTSup 373 (London: Sheffield Academic Press, 2003).

6 Richard Layard, 'Happiness: has social science a clue?', Lionel Robbins Memorial Lecture, March 2003, p. 14. See <http://cep.lse.ac.uk/events/lectures/layard/RL030303.pdf>.

7 See further in Mark Green, *The Best Idea in the World* (Grand Rapids: Zondervan, 2009).

8 Caroline Hocking, 'Cold turkey for a Facebook addict'. See <http://news.bbc.co.uk/1/hi/magazine/8299362.stm>.

3 Time is money?

1 This 'modern parable' is a rendition of a much older one.

2 Michael Schluter, 'Time and priorities', 2005. See <http://www.jubilee-centre.org/document.php?id=138>.

3 Eric Zencey, 'G.D.P. R.I.P.' in the *New York Times*, 9 August 2009. See <http://www.nytimes.com/2009/08/10/opinion/10zencey.html>.

4 Bill Bryson, *Made in America* (London: Secker & Warburg, 1994), p. 276.

5 A 2007 survey suggested that today's mothers do around half as much housework as in the 1970s (<http://www.dailymail.co.uk/news/article-487159/Women-hours-housework-week--half-30-years-ago.html>). However, modern men are not picking up the difference; another survey of 28 countries found that men did an average of 9.41 hours of housework per week and women an average of 21.13. See <http://www.timesonline.co.uk/tol/life_and_style/men/article2241733.ece>.

6 'Nation of TV addicts watch for longer than they work', *The Independent*, 19 May 2000. See <http://www.independent.co.uk/news/media/nation-of-tv-addicts-watch-for-longer-than-they-work-718937.html>.

7 Benjamin Franklin, *Advice to a Young Tradesman* (Philadelphia, 1748).

8 Lisa Lerer, 'The scourge of the billable hour', *Slate* magazine. See <http://www.slate.com/id/2180420/>.

9 The system of dividing the hours of daylight into 12 was known in Egypt and other Ancient Near Eastern civilizations. Since the concept of an hour apparently enters biblical thought somewhere between the Testaments, it seems fair to assume that it was imported from Greek or Roman thought, in the same way that the four watches of the night (Mark 6.48; 13.35) instead of the Jewish three were a Roman feature.

10 It's possible that some shorter-term crisis, such as persecution or the grain famine of the AD 40s and 50s (see Acts 11.27–28), added to Paul's sense of urgency.

11 See Paul Shepanski and Michael Diamond, 'An unexpected tragedy: evidence for the connection between working patterns and family breakdown in Australia' (Relationships Forum, Australia, 2007). See <http://www.relationshipsfoundation.org/download.php?id=167>.

12 Friedrich Nietzsche, *Beyond Good and Evil*, §189.

13 Talmud tractate *Shabbat*, 14.

14 See further in Michael Schluter, 'Roots: biblical norm or cultural anachronism?', *Cambridge Papers*, vol. 4, no. 4, December 1995. See <http://www.jubilee-centre.org/document.php?id=12&topicID=0>.

15 See <http://www.contractjournal.com/blogs/brickonomics/2009/01/ plunging-sales-rates-in-2008-a.html>.

16 From Zelda West-Meads, *To Love, Honour and Betray* (London: Hodder & Stoughton, 1997), pp. 70–3.

17 *Midrash Leviticus Rabbah*, 18.1.

4 Selling sex

1 'Thrill of the chaste', *The Observer*, 26 October 2008. See <http:// www.guardian.co.uk:80/lifeandstyle/2008/oct/26/period-of-celibacy>.

2 Office for National Statistics, 'Marriages', 2007 figures – see <http:// www.statistics.gov.uk/cci/nugget.asp?id=322>.

3 Office for National Statistics, 'Divorces', 2007 figures – see <http:// www.statistics.gov.uk/cci/nugget.asp?id=170>.

4 See 'Abortion statistics, England and Wales: 2007', at <http:// www.dh.gov.uk/en/Publicationsandstatistics/Publications/ PublicationsStatistics/DH_085508>.

5 Cohabitation is not a new phenomenon. Before the Marriage Act of 1753, the lines between marriage and cohabitation ('common-law marriage') were blurred. What is new is that cohabitation is being chosen specifically as an alternative to marriage, not effectively a different form of the same thing.

6 Dale Kuehne, *Sex and the iWorld: Rethinking Relationship Beyond an Age of Individualism* (Grand Rapids: Baker Academic, 2009), pp. 35, 38, 41.

7 Kuehne, *Sex and the iWorld*, pp. 43–4.

8 Christopher Ash, *Marriage: Sex in the service of God* (Leicester: Inter-Varsity Press, 2003), pp. 63–5.

9 See Guy Brandon, *Just Sex: Is it Ever Just Sex?* (Nottingham: Inter-Varsity Press, 2009), Appendix.

10 'Breast practice on the riviera', see <http://news.bbc.co.uk/1/hi/world/ europe/8178818.stm>.

11 Wendy Shalit, *A Return to Modesty* (New York: Free Press, 1999), p. 54.

12 Harriet Harman, quoted at <http://www.equalities.gov.uk/media_zone/ press_releases/women_not_for_sale.aspx>.

13 See Brandon, *Just Sex*, p. 111 and Appendix, nos 4–13.

14 See Jonathan Burnside, 'Consent versus community: what basis for sexual offences?' (Cambridge: Jubilee Centre, 2006), pp. 1–3. See <http://www.jubilee-centre.org/uploaded/files/resource_75.pdf>.

15 Personal exchange.

16 See e.g. 'Absent fathers and social breakdown go together like smoking and cancer' in the *Telegraph* blogs, 13 July 2009. See <http://blogs. telegraph.co.uk:80/news/edwest/100003046/absent-fathers-and-social-breakdown-go-together-like-smoking-and-cancer/>. For a broad picture of effects, see 'Experiments in living: the fatherless family', Civitas, summary at <http://www.civitas.org.uk/pubs/ experiments.php>.

17 Lynda Clarke and Ann Berrington, 'Socio-Demographic Predictors of Divorce', in *High Divorce Rates: The State of the Evidence on Reasons and Remedies*, vol. 1 (London: Lord Chancellor's Department, Research Secretariat, 1999).

18 Personal exchange.

19 Peter Lynas, 'When relationships go wrong: counting the cost of family failure', Relationships Foundation, see <http:// www.relationshipsfoundation.org/download.php?id=246>.

20 For more detailed figures, see Brandon, *Just Sex*, pp. 134–6.

21 See e.g. John Stuart Mill, *On Liberty* (London, 1859), pp. 21–2.

22 For more on the relational and financial impacts of different sexual relationships, see Brandon, *Just Sex*, chapters 2 and 5.

23 Christopher J. H. Wright, *Old Testament Ethics for the People of God* (Leicester: Inter-Varsity Press, 2004), p. 363.

24 Wright, *Old Testament Ethics*, p. 364.

25 C. S. Lewis, *The Four Loves* (London: Geoffrey Bles, 1960).

5 Just shopping

1 'Consumers have "too many choices"', BBC News, see <http:// news.bbc.co.uk/1/hi/uk/724080.stm>.

2 Despite the recession, UK Fairtrade sales increased to around £700 million in 2008 (from £493 million in 2007). See <http://www.tradingvisions.org/ node/67>. Globally, consumers bought €2.9 billion of Fairtrade products, an increase of 22 per cent compared with 2007. See <http:// www.fairtrade.org.uk/press_office/press_releases_and_statements/ jun_2009/global_fairtrade_sales_increase_by_22.aspx>.

3 'Greener by miles', the *Daily Telegraph*, 3 June 2007. See <http://www. telegraph.co.uk/news/uknews/1553456/Greener-by-miles.html>.

4 How much, it is hard to say; a like-for-like comparison is difficult because the choice is rarely between two identical types of coffee of the same quality and origin with identical production and transport costs.

5 Cf. Marc Sidwell, 'Unfair Trade' (London: Adam Smith Institute, 2008), pp. 3, 11, 28. See <http://www.adamsmith.org/images/pdf/ unfair_trade.pdf>.

6 See <www.befair.be/site/download.cfm?SAVE=1314&LG=1>. 'Fair Trade' here, and so written, refers to FINE's agreed (in 2001) definition and principles. FINE is a loose association of the four largest fair-trade networks, one of which is FLO, Fairtrade Labelling Organizations International, which regulates the Fairtrade brand itself (the 'FINE' acronym is composed of the first letters of the four networks).

7 From *The Guardian*, 'Teach us how to fish – do not just give us the fish', 12 March 2008. See <http://www.guardian.co.uk/environment/2008/mar/12/ethicalliving.lifeandhealth>.

8 See <http://www.fairtrade.org.uk/press_office/press_releases_and_statements/jun_2009/global_fairtrade_sales_increase_by_22.aspx>.

9 See <http://business.timesonline.co.uk/tol/business/industry_sectors/article6531246.ece>.

10 Found at <http://thrakika.gr/en/news/detail.php?NEWS_ID=5193&phrase_id=17179&print=Y>.

11 See <http://news.bbc.co.uk/1/hi/uk/8407289.stm>.

12 See BBC clip at <http://news.bbc.co.uk/1/hi/uk/8409253.stm>.

13 See Appendix 2, note 1.

14 See <http://www.fairtrade.org.uk/press_office/press_releases_and_statements/archive_2007/dec_2007/small_scale_coffee_farmers_to_benefit_from_international_increase_in_fairtrade_price.aspx>.

15 See <http://www.starbucks.com/sharedplanet/ethicalInternal.aspx?story=pricesAndQuality>.

16 Also look out for 4C Association, Cup of Excellence, and Utz Certified, Allegro Coffee and Intelligentsia Coffee.

17 See <http://www.stopthetraffik.org/chocolateDownloads/chocolate_guide_uk.pdf>.

18 'Greener by miles'.

19 'Tesco takes "local" chicken on 1,000 mile trip', the *Daily Telegraph*, 20 March 2008. See <http://www.telegraph.co.uk/news/uknews/1582202/Tesco-takes-'local'-chickens-on-1,000-mile-trip.html>.

20 See <http://www.wrap.org.uk/retail/food_waste/>.

21 'Organic pigs breed more bad bugs', *New Scientist*, 24 June 2008. See <http://www.newscientist.com/channel/health/mg19826613.000-organic-pigs-breed-more-bad-bugs.html>.

22 For a broader discussion of ethical arguments around Genetic Engineering, see Denis Alexander, 'Genetic engineering in God's world', *Cambridge Papers*, vol. 6, no. 2, June 1997. See <http://www.jubilee-centre.org/document.php?id=17>.

23 'Suddenly being green is not cool any more', *The Times*, 7 August 2008. See <http://www.timesonline.co.uk/tol/comment/columnists/guest_contributors/article4474202.ece>.

6 Social footprint: our environmental imprint

1 See <http://www.theonion.com/content/node/48972>.
2 See, for example, the reports of the IPCC on its website – <http://www.ipcc.ch/> – and the Stern Review – <http://www.occ.gov.uk/activities/stern.htm>.
3 See <http://www.nationalpost.com/news/story.html?id=164002>.
4 Robert White, 'A burning issue: Christian care for the environment', *Cambridge Papers*, vol. 15, no. 4, December 2006. See <http://www.jubilee-centre.org/document.php?id=53>.
5 Nick Spencer and Robert White, *Christianity, Climate Change and Sustainable Living* (London: SPCK, 2007), p. 49.
6 See BP's annual *Statistical Review of World Energy*, www.bp.com. It does not take into account other sources such as oil sands, which cannot be mined under current economic and technological conditions but might come to play a greater role as other reserves are depleted.
7 Energy consumption also broadly reflects fossil fuel use and therefore carbon emissions too, though some variations are caused by power sources and efficiency. So industry and service were responsible for around 46 per cent of carbon emissions in 2000, whereas domestic and transport were responsible for 28 per cent and 26 per cent respectively. Spencer and White, *Christianity, Climate Change and Sustainable Living*, p. 53.
8 DTI/ONS, see Spencer and White, *Christianity, Climate Change and Sustainable Living*, p. 55.
9 Leo Hickman, *A Good Life* (London: Eden Project Books, 2005), pp. 86–7.
10 Spencer and White, *Christianity, Climate Change and Sustainable Living*, pp. 58–9.
11 See <http://www.sustainable-development.gov.uk/sustainable/quality04/maind/04d15.htm>.
12 See <http://www.statistics.gov.uk/cci/nugget.asp?id=1096>.
13 Credit Action figures for August 2009. See <http://www.creditaction.org.uk/debt-statistics.html>. The figure of £21,500 is the average for households that actually have unsecured debt, not for all households.
14 'The impact of UK households on the environment through direct and indirect generation of greenhouse gases' (London: Office for National Statistics, 2004). See <http://www.statistics.gov.uk/downloads/theme_environment/Impact_of_households_final_report.pdf>.
15 Cf. 'Standby buttons face axe to curb energy waste', *Sunday Times*, 9 July 2006. See <http://www.timesonline.co.uk/tol/news/uk/article685096.ece>.

16 See <http://www.berr.gov.uk/files/file11250.pdf>, p. 27.
17 'Solo living's eco threat', *The Guardian*, 1 August 2006. See <http://www.guardian.co.uk/environment/2006/aug/01/money.ethicalmoney>.
18 From Nick Totton, 'In defence of dependency', *Therapy Today*, June 2006. Totton's figures are from Robert W. Poole Jr and C. Kenneth Orski, 'HOT Lanes: a better way to attack urban highway congestion', *Regulation* (Spring 2000), vol. 23, no. 1, pp. 15–20 (see <http://www.cato.org/pubs/regulation/regv23n1/poole.pdf>).
19 Kinetic's Moving World research, 2007, cf. <http://www.mediaweek.co.uk/news/851688/Commuters---Research---Commuters-microscope/>.
20 'Commuters' journeys are getting longer', *The Times*, 31 August 2007. See <http://www.timesonline.co.uk/tol/news/uk/article2358053.ece>.
21 'Meat by numbers', *The Observer*, 7 September 2008. See <http://www.guardian.co.uk/environment/2008/sep/07/food.beef>.
22 'Half of UK don't know their neighbours', *Mail Online*, 15 August 2005. See <http://www.dailymail.co.uk/news/article-359343/Half-UK-dont-know-neigbours.html>.
23 Comment from BBC website. See <http://news.bbc.co.uk/1/hi/world/africa/4171669.stm>.
24 Stern Review, executive summary, p. vi. See <http://www.hm-treasury.gov.uk/d/CLOSED_SHORT_executive_summary.pdf>.
25 'World is facing a natural resources crisis worse than financial crunch', *The Guardian*, 29 October 2008. See <http://www.guardian.co.uk/environment/2008/oct/29/climatechange-endangeredhabitats>.
26 White, 'A burning issue'.

7 Worship with wealth

1 See <http://www.globalrichlist.com>.
2 A fuller treatment of the biblical economy is given in Michael Schluter and John Ashcroft (eds), *Jubilee Manifesto: A Framework, Agenda and Strategy for Christian Social Reform* (Leicester: Inter-Varsity Press, 2005), chapter 12.
3 My translation.
4 From <http://www.bbc.co.uk/wales/x-ray/sites/allarticles/updates/090624_loan_sharks.shtml>.
5 Paul Mills, 'Interest in interest: the Old Testament ban on interest and its implications for today' (Cambridge: Jubilee Centre, 1989), p. 31.
6 Mills, 'Interest in interest', pp. 28–9.
7 See also the parable of the talents (Matt. 25.14–30).
8 There is evidence that the interest-based system has the effect of exaggerating economic cycles; in times of prosperity companies are

incentivized to borrow more heavily to finance their business because they can easily meet the fixed repayments. When there is a downturn, the payments do not change but they are less able to meet them.

9 See 2009 budget documents at <http://news.bbc.co.uk/1/hi/business/8012222.stm>.

10 See <http://www.telegraph.co.uk/finance/financetopics/budget/5202037/Britains-national-debt-to-reach-1.4-trillion-under-2009-Budget.html>.

11 Schluter and Ashcroft (eds), *Jubilee Manifesto*, p. 200.

12 Excluding mortgage debt, which tends to be at a relatively low interest rate.

13 Michael Schluter, 'Risk, reward and responsibility: limited liability and company reform', *Cambridge Papers*, vol. 9, no. 2, June 2000, p. 2.

14 See <http://news.scotsman.com/farepak/A-year-gone-but-still.3470355.jp>.

15 Economic growth is not a zero-sum game; there is an increasing amount of wealth in the world. However, when gain is realized – i.e. something is sold – someone has to pay for it.

16 Andrew Hartropp, *What is Economic Justice? Biblical and Secular Perspectives Contrasted* (Milton Keynes: Paternoster, 2007), p. 161.

17 Gary North, *An Introduction to Christian Economics* (Nutley, NJ: Craig Press, 1973), p. 197.

18 Deut. 24.14–15; Jer. 22.13.

19 Jer. 17.11.

20 Ezek. 22.12–13.

21 Lev. 19.35–36; Deut. 25.13–16.

22 Amos 8.4–6.

23 See 'International Food Policy Research Institute Forum: Speculation and world food markets', August 2008, at <http://www.ifpri.org/publication/ifpri-forum-speculation-and-world-food-markets>.

24 For those interested in game theory, this is an example of a Nash Equilibrium; both participants know the other's investment strategy, and neither will benefit from changing their own strategy in the light of this information.

25 In *Bild*, April 2005. Reference from <http://www.bbc.co.uk/blogs/thereporters/robertpeston/2008/10/hedge_funds_and_vw_what_a_pile.html>.

26 Note that he already had barns in which he could have stored some of the harvest; we are not forbidden from having some cash to hand, only from keeping an unnecessarily large proportion of our assets in liquid form.

27 Quoted in Edward W. Bauman, *Where Your Treasure Is* (Arlington, VA: Bauman Bible Telecasts, 1980), p. 74. Reference found in Richard J.

Foster, *Money, Sex and Power: The Challenge to the Disciplined Life* (London: Hodder & Stoughton, 1985), p. 43.

28 Simon Guillebaud, *For What It's Worth* (Oxford: Monarch Books, 2006), p. 156.

29 In fact penalties for overpaying sometimes make this uneconomical.

30 Where it is economical, an integrated mortgage may be one way of achieving this. Savings are offset against mortgage debt, so mortgage payments are reduced (at the expense of receiving interest on the savings). This has the biblically desirable effect of reducing both interest paid and received – rather than taking out a large loan at interest, and holding separate savings at interest – and the financial advantages of reducing mortgage payments and retaining liquidity. However, rates tend to be slightly higher than conventional mortgages, so a reasonably large amount of savings may be required to make the difference worthwhile.

31 The FTSE4Good index is one starting point for socially responsible investing; however, there are other factors beyond the ethical criteria used to include companies, such as deciding the legitimacy of owning shares in the first place and the degree of responsibility taken and influence over the company.

32 Such as Zopa – see <http://uk.zopa.com> or <http://us.zopa.com>, Virgin Money US – see <http://www.virginmoneyus.com/PersonalLoans/tabid/54/Default.aspx>, and many others.

8 Spiritual health

1 From *Yes!* magazine, '10 things science says will make you happy', 31 October, 2008. See <http://www.yesmagazine.org/issues/sustainable-happiness/10-things-science-says-will-make-you>.

2 C. S. Lewis, *The Problem of Pain* (London: Centenary Press, 1940), p. 104.

3 John Coffey, 'Engaging with cinema', *Cambridge Papers*, vol. 8, no. 1, March 1999. Available at <http://www.jubilee-centre.org/document.php?id=23#_edn4>.

4 Coffey, 'Engaging with cinema'.

5 Fr Timothy V. Vavarek, 'Christian asceticism: breaking consumerism's destructive hold', in the *Houston Catholic Worker*, vol. 21, no. 1, 2001.

6 Michael Schluter and David Lee, *The R Option: Building Relationships as a Better Way of Life* (Cambridge: The Relationships Foundation, 2003), p. 20. In fact Gallup's tombstone reads: 'BE BOLDE // BE WYSE'.

7 Graham Cray, *Disciples and Citizens* (Nottingham: Inter-Varsity Press, 2007), p. 9.

9 Conclusion: whole-life discipleship

1 Simon Guillebaud, *For What It's Worth* (Oxford: Monarch Books, 2006), pp. 36–7.

Appendix 1: Background to the financial crisis

1 Around 5 million people are claiming some sort of out-of-work benefit.

Appendix 2: The complexities of Fairtrade

1 The Fairtrade Foundation is the UK 'Labelling Initiative' affiliated to FLO that licenses use of the Fairtrade mark on products sold in the UK – see also Chapter 5, note 6.

2 'TransFair USA, the US 'Labelling Initiative' affiliated to FLO, reports that of the 170 million pounds of fair trade coffee produced globally, only 35 million pounds are sold on the market.' See <http://www.transfairusa.org/content/about/archives_news/n_060524.php>. See also <http://coopcoffees.com/all_news/media/articles/fair-trade-or-fairly-traded/>.

3 See FLO-CERT website, <http://www.flo-cert.net/flo-cert/main.php?lg=en>.

4 Personal correspondence.

5 Alex Singleton, 'The Poverty of Fairtrade Coffee', in the *Telegraph*, 23 February 2008. See <http://blogs.telegraph.co.uk/alex_singleton/blog/2008/02/23/the_poverty_of_fairtrade_coffee>.

6 Richard Lipsey and K. Alex Chrystal, *Economics*, 11th edn (Oxford: Oxford University Press, 2007), pp. 80–1.

All URLs correct as of 1 December 2009.

Further reading

Ash, Christopher, *Marriage: Sex in the Service of God* (Leicester: Inter-Varsity Press, 2003).

Brandon, Guy, *Just Sex: Is it Ever Just Sex?* (Nottingham: Inter-Varsity Press, 2009). See particularly the appendix for a discussion of answers to common questions about biblical sexual ethics.

Cray, Graham, *Disciples and Citizens* (Nottingham: Inter-Varsity Press, 2007).

Greene, Mark, *The Best Idea in the World* (Grand Rapids, Mich.: Zondervan, 2009).

Guillebaud, Simon, *For What It's Worth* (Oxford: Monarch Books, 2006).

Hickman, Leo, *A Good Life* (London: Eden Project Books, 2005).

Kuehne, Dale, *Sex and the iWorld: Rethinking Relationship Beyond an Age of Individualism* (Grand Rapids, Mich.: Baker Academic, 2009).

Lynas, Rose (ed.), *Votewise Now! Helping Christians Engage with the Issues* (London: SPCK, 2009).

Mills, Paul, 'Interest in interest: the Old Testament ban on interest and its implications for today' (Cambridge: Jubilee Centre, 1989).

Mills, Paul, 'Investing as a Christian: reaping where you have not sown?', *Cambridge Papers*, vol. 5, no. 2, June 1996.

Schluter, Michael and John Ashcroft (eds), *Jubilee Manifesto: A Framework, Agenda and Strategy for Christian Social Reform* (Leicester: Inter-Varsity Press, 2005).

Schluter, Michael and David Lee, *The R Option: Building Relationships as a Better Way of Life* (Cambridge: Relationships Foundation, 2003), pp. 63–73.

Shalit, Wendy, *A Return to Modesty: Discovering the Lost Virtue* (New York: Free Press, 1999).

Spencer, Nick and Robert White, *Christianity, Climate Change and Sustainable Living* (London: SPCK, 2007).

White, Robert, 'A burning issue: Christian care for the environment', *Cambridge Papers*, vol. 15, no. 4, December 2006.

Wright, Christopher, *Old Testament Ethics for the People of God* (Leicester: Inter-Varsity Press, 2004).